A SCHOOL OF DOLPHINS
The History of The Godolphin and Latymer School

FRANCHA LEALE TOGE.

A SCHOOL OF DOLPHINS

The History of The Godolphin and Latymer School

Sally Holloway

The Book Guild Ltd
Sussex, England

The Book Guild Ltd
25 High Street,
Lewes, Sussex

First published 1995
© The Governors of Godolphin and Latymer School and
Sally Holloway 1995
Set in Bembo
Typesetting by Acorn Bookwork, Salisbury, Wiltshire

Printed in Great Britain by
Bookcraft (Bath) Ltd

A catalogue record for this book is available from the
British Library

ISBN 1 85776 090 5

CONTENTS

LIST OF ILLUSTRATIONS

COLOUR PLATES

Four of the School's Head Mistresses from 1935–1990: (l to r) Barbara Dean, Margaret Gray, Margaret Rudland and Dame Joyce Bishop

Young ladies of the Latymer and Hammersmith Female Charity School – 1840s

Dolphins in uniform – a varied species

GALUP 'DIY Demo Kit' poster, for march on Parliament – 1975

90 years on – Godolphin and Latymer staff – 1995 (Courtesy Gillman & Soame, Oxford)

Misty morning bird's eye view of the new Science/Arts block under construction – 1990 (Courtesy John Stratta)

Exhibition in new Art room, 1995

Hockey and tennis on the field

Rowing on the Thames above Hammersmith Bridge – 1995

Roll Up! Roll Up! at the Lyric, Hammersmith, 1995

Science for juniors – and seniors

Fourteen-year-old LVs in the University courtyard at Salamanca

Crema

Zagorsk

Sinai desert

Our oldest exchange with our friends at the Johanneum, Hamburg

Dedicated to the continued survival, success and contentment of all Dolphins – throughout the world.

PREFACE AND ACKNOWLEDGMENTS

In researching this book I have had, as always, kindness and the most friendly and willing help from everyone in Godolphin and Latymer as well as many people beyond its walls. To all of them, I offer my thanks, but in particular to Lady Goodison, James Macnair, George Nissen and all the Governors who trusted me with the commission and who have supported me with the utmost kindness. Margaret Rudland has generously given up time – both on and off duty – to helping whenever I have asked (which was quite frequently) and to her, my special thanks as, indeed, to Margaret Gray and Beryl Viner, whose combined experience goes back to the early days of World War Two and has been immensely valuable.

My gratitude also to Colin Diggory, the Headmaster, and to the Governors of Latymer Upper School for allowing me to research in their archives, and to Christopher Hammond and Kate Pestkowska for their assistance. Colonel Alex Menzies, Clerk to the Governors of Godolphin and Latymer, has willingly and cheerfully delved into our legal past at my request and emerged with many items of interest, not least all the surviving Minutes both of the Godolphin School for Boys and our own School. And my gratitude also to Gillian Low for being always there and quietly ready to help.

From Godolphin House at Breage, Cornwall, Mrs Mary Schofield has been generous in providing information about the Godolphin family, and Mrs Hilary Fender, Head Mistress of The Godolphin School, Salisbury, has received my inquiries with friendly interest and enthusiasm.

My thanks, also, in no significant order for they have all been equally kind, to Christine Bayliss and Anne Wheeldon, archivists at Hammersmith Council Archives Department; Sheila Rose, whose book on Dame Joyce Bishop I have raided with her blessings; to Gladys Southgate (née Killick) and to Jennifer Watson; Doris and Irene Conrady, Phyllis Dunning (née Morgan), Caroline Shattock and more helpful Old Dolphins than I have space to mention; Heather Rossotti, Bursar; Rosemary Vercoe, Honorary Secretary of Hammersmith Historical Society; John Stratta for providing photographs (not only those which had been hoarded in the roof space but others which he had taken himself); also to Berenice Goodwin for her help with photography; to the School Librarian, Linda Matthews, and the Assistant Librarian, Ann Longrigg; to Vivienne Cox and the cheerful crew in the School Office (the tea was much appreciated!).

Among the teaching staff, the Head of English, Pamela Shadlock; Mathematics: Amanda Atherton; History: Quintin Davies; Geography: Jane

Blower; Modern Languages: Deborah Dawe; Economics: Pauline Lightfoot; Music: John Escott; Physical Education: Jenny Mitchell; Science: Judith Field; Classics: Wendy Yeats; Religious Studies: Kenneth Wolfe; Drama: Mick Fitzmaurice; Art: Berenice Goodwin; Home Economics: Elizabeth Foster; as well as Ann Frost (Spanish); Paulette Ranaraja (French); Svetlana Andreyeva (Russian); Sue Adey (PE); Matilda Cockbain (History); Edna Pearson (Catering); Joan Elleboode.

At The Book Guild, I value the professionalism and patience of Carol Biss and the staff, particularly my copy editor, Sheila Lynford.

Not least, my love and thanks to David, who, as always, was a constant support and adviser.

Sally Holloway
Barnes, 1995

BRIEF HISTORICAL SUMMARY

THE GODOLPHIN FOUNDATION

1696   Date of Sir William Godolphin's will, by which he bequeathed certain sums of money for charitable uses.

1703   Ground purchased by Elizabeth Godolphin, one of the two residuary legatees, on the west side of St James's Street, Piccadilly. This was then let on a building lease at a rent of £45 per annum.

1852   The Charity Commission made a scheme appropriating the whole of the income of the St James's Street houses for educational purposes.

1856   On this income the Godolphin School for Boys was opened in Great Church Lane, Hammersmith.

1861   The present site in Iffley Road was purchased for £800. The foundation stone was laid on 8 June (Founder's Day) by Dr Archibald Campbell Tait, Bishop of London.

1900   The Godolphin School closed.

THE LATYMER FOUNDATION

1624   Date of Mr Edward Latymer's will, directing that certain lands be held in trust for the poor of Hammersmith and to the end that deserving boys could be put to school to keep them from vagrant courses.

1756   The Latymer Foundation School erected.

1800s   Girls attended the Latymer and Hammersmith Charity School.

1894   Latymer Upper School founded under a new scheme and opened by Dr Temple, Bishop of London.

THE GODOLPHIN AND LATYMER FOUNDATION

1903   Order made establishing scheme for joint foundation as a girls' school.

1905   Godolphin and Latymer School opened on 4 May with 67 pupils in temporary premises at 251 King Street, W6.

1906   In January, the School moved into converted buildings of the old Godolphin School for Boys with 205 pupils. The new buildings were opened by the Duke of Leeds.

1909	Further extensions opened to accommodate 500 pupils. The first gym was built on the site of the boys' chapel. Biology, chemistry and general laboratories built. The Art Room was established on the north side of the first floor. Rooms 13, 14, 15, 16, 17, 18 and 19 were added, plus the Staff Room.
1913	Organ built by Harrison & Harrison in memory of Mr Thomas Chamberlen, first Chairman of the Governing body.
1914	Winterstoke Scholarship founded by Miss Stancomb Wills in memory of her uncle, Lord Winterstoke, a former Governor of the School.
1918	School roof damaged by shell in First World War.
1921	School Magazine started.
1927	Godolphin Library opened to commemorate 21st birthday of the School.
1928	Physics laboratory built.
1931	Franc Ha Leal Fund started.
1935	Head Mistress's house converted into a house for the Preparatory Department.
1936	Domestic Science room built.
1937	Library reading room built with memorial to Miss Zachary.
1939	World War Two started, School evacuated to Ascot and later to Newbury.
1940	Gymnasium damaged by bomb during London blitz.
1943	School returned to Iffley Road
1945	Parent-Teacher Association started
1950	New gymnasium built. Closure of Preparatory Department. Head Mistress's House used for coaching rooms, secretarial VIth form and pottery classes.
1951	School received voluntary aided status.
1955	School Jubilee celebrated.
1956	Changing rooms and showers built.
1957	Medical rooms and games pavilion built.
1959	Extensions to staff room and Cloakroom A.
1960	Demolition of Head Mistress's house and a three-storey Science building erected on the site.
1961	Opening of the new Science block, the Gryphon Library and other reconstructed rooms.
1967	Construction of a two-storey block housing the Music and Art Departments and a VIth form common room.
1971	Cloister area glazed, staff dining room created. Inner courtyard repaved.

1977   In September the School reverted to its original independent status.

1984   Refurbishment of the Victorian sick bay and staff dormitory accommodation and part of the roof into classrooms, laboratory, a Careers room and Resources room. The Gryphon Library converted into the Computer room.

1987   Refurbishment of the organ by Harrison & Harrison Ltd.

1991   New three-storey Art, Science and Technology Building and the Dean Library opened by the Rt Hon. Christopher Patten, MP, on 14 March on site of former Art, Music and VIth form building. Library altered to accommodate Dean Library.

HEAD MISTRESSES

1905–18	Miss Gertrude Clement, B.A.
1919–35	Miss Katharine Zachary, B.A.
1935–63	Dame Joyce Bishop, D.B.E., M.A.
1963–73	Miss Margaret Gray, M.A.
1974–85	Miss Barbara Dean, M.A.
1986–	Miss Margaret Rudland, B.Sc.

CHAIRMEN OF THE GOVERNORS

1905–12	Thomas Chamberlen, Esq
1912–22	The Bishop of Worcester
1922–25	J Glasier, Esq
1925–31	Sir William Bull Bt, MP
1931–48	Sir Marshall Hays, JP
1948–61	Lady Moberly, M.A.
1961–79	Lady Brooke of Cumnor, D.B.E.
1979–83	Miss Janet Glover, C.B.E., M.A.
1983–	Lady Goodison

1

THE WILL OF GODOLPHIN

The Godolphin family had lived in Cornwall since before the Norman Conquest, under a variety of names – Godollon, Godolcan, Godolghan, Godwolghan – until the records show, in 1050, the name of John de Godolphin. The meaning of the name is lost in time. According to Marion Smith, who wrote a history of the family and its home, Godolphin House at Breage near Helston, it might have had a geographical root – 'rising ground' or 'little hill'. Earlier, others had suggested 'white eagle'. Certainly the emblem which they chose was a white eagle – possibly brought back by one of the family warriors who had fought through Europe and taken for his own the popular white, double-headed eagle of Charlemagne, which, it was said, looked from east to west to symbolise his empire on which the sun never set. Their crest, worn on top of their helmets to identify them in battle, was a pun on their name – a dolphin.

For their motto, suitably reflecting the years in which they had guarded their rocky coasts to ensure that they remained free to lead their lives in the way they wished, underlining their independence and loyalty to those around them, they chose the old Cornish tongue, rooted in ancient French. Its exact spelling has been lost in the ensuing centuries but, according to the Cornish Language Council, one of several possibilities is '*Francha leale toge*' (pronounced 'frank ha leal ertoji'). Translated, it means 'Free and loyal art thou'.

By the mid-seventeenth century their home, Godolphin, was based near Helston and the family was one of the most powerful and respected in the country. They had amassed a considerable fortune from their local mines and in 1634 William Godolphin was born in the family house. (The names William, Francis and Sidney were constantly repeated, causing confusion to future historians.) This William joined Westminster School as a King's Scholar in 1645 when he was eleven years old, and went on to Christ Church, Oxford when he was seventeen. He studied law and practised as a barrister before entering the first Restoration Parliament in 1661 as the MP for Camelford in Cornwall. He was sent to Madrid in 1665 and studied Castilian law there, as well as negotiating a treaty which ended all Spanish pretensions to Jamaica and the West Indian Islands and secured other advantages for British commerce. The Treaty was hailed as 'a triumph of diplomatic skill'. Godolphin was knighted by Charles II and returned to Madrid first as

Sir William Godolphin (Courtesy, Manchester City Art Gallery)

Envoy Extraordinary (1669) then Ambassador (1671).

Samuel Pepys, who had survived the Great Fire of London and socialised among the highest in the land, described William in his diary: 'I do find him a very pretty and able person, a man of very fine parts – as wise and able a person as any prince in the world hath'. (A copy of the extract, in Pepys' personal 'shorthand', hangs in the School cloisters.)

Pretty and able he may have been, but by the time of his last journey to Madrid he was also a very sick man and, in the constant care of Jesuit priests, he was believed to have embraced the Roman Catholic faith. England at that time was a fiercely Protestant country and 'Papists' received short shrift at the hands of the population. The trial of the famous Catholic Titus Oates in 1671 coincided with the reports of Godolphin's conversion. Parliament petitioned the King to recall him from Madrid and charge him with high treason. He was, in fact, deprived of his office but stayed in Madrid until his death in 1696.

Sir William was a bachelor who had during his lifetime made three different wills. The first left £3,000 of his £80,000 fortune to be devoted to charitable causes. Following his illness, he wrote a second will, leaving his entire fortune to the Jesuits for the good of his soul. Then, shortly before his death, he wrote a third will in which he left his fortune to his nephew and niece, Francis and Elizabeth Godolphin.

When the family sought to claim back his estates from Spain, the Jesuits stepped in to contest the will and the quarrel was finally decided by the House of Commons, which declared, in 1698, that the second will had been written under undue influence. Instead, they combined the provisions of the first and third wills, and passed an Act of Parliament (9 & 10 William III, c19) under which Francis and Elizabeth became residuary legatees, conditional upon their each devoting £1,520 to charitable causes.

Francis died before he could take any action. Elizabeth Godolphin lived on but her husband and cousin, Charles Godolphin, seems to have managed her affairs. He spent £500 for the benefit of Helston and bought two houses in St James's Street, Westminster, with the remaining £1,000. These were assigned by deed to trustees and the income from their rents was to be used 'for the education and maintenance of poor scholars, the relief of decayed virtuous gentlemen, the redemption of prisoners and the placing out of poor children to trades, or other such like pious and charitable uses'.

(Elizabeth also used some of her own private income to found the Godolphin School for Girls in Salisbury, but this was not part of Sir William's legacy.)

The family name became famous later for introducing the Godolphin Arab, a breed of horse which became one of the founders of English racing bloodstock. But little was heard of the Charity until 1787, when the management of the Trust was put into the care of the Godolphin heirs after proceedings in Chancery, and there it stayed for nearly half a century.

In 1819 the first Charity Commission was established, and among the 'forgotten' bequests which they inquired into was that of Sir William Godolphin. The only surviving trustee appeared to be a Mr Robert Long, a solicitor, who failed to respond to the Commissioners' requests for information. The case of HM Attorney General v. Long dragged through Chancery for 17 years until, in 1852, the Court declared that the accumulated money should be devoted 'to the maintenance of a School in the county of Middlesex ... and the accumulated funds to the erection of suitable buildings'. Trustees were appointed, the School was to be advertised and anyone who felt it would be of value to their area could apply.

Godolphin House, Cornwall

2

DOLPHIN BOYS

On 8 March 1855 the first meeting of the Trustees of the Godolphin School for Boys was held.

The Minutes of that meeting record that a Headmaster, the Rev. Henry Twells, M.A., plus a Second Master were appointed and a Clerk to the Trustees who was instructed 'to purchase proper books for the use of the Trustees and a fireproof box to put them in'. (The books survive, but not the box.)

The Clerk was also asked to look round 'for the best locality for a School and House to be hired... among incumbents of the populous Parishes and Districts of the County of Middlesex, situate in the neighbourhood of London'.

Although one might have thought that the next meeting of the Trustees was rather important, too few turned up to form a quorum (of three). Nevertheless, the Clerk reported that he had bought the fireproof box and the books and that every suitable parish had been asked for information on a possible site in their area. Replies had been sent offering land in Islington, Highbury, Shoreditch, Haggerston and Hackney, but all had schools established already in their areas. The Vicar of Hammersmith, however, had written suggesting a house in Great Church Lane, close to the Broadway (slightly north of the present Talgarth Road). There were no competing schools in the area so the search was concentrated there.

It was in Great Burlington House, previously used as a small private school, that the Trustees opened the Godolphin School for Boys on 5 August 1856. As Headmaster the Rev. Henry Twells, M.A., of St Peter's College, Cambridge, would receive a salary of £100 plus an extra payment for each boy in the school, the Second Master, Mr John Rice of Pembroke College Oxford would receive £60. Three Godolphin Scholars would be appointed (as funds allowed!) at £24 each.

By October 1847 the new school had 47 pupils, 10 boarders and 37 day boys, and fees were £6 a year. More boys were applying but were 'declined on the grounds that they cannot read or write'. The report to the Trustees suggests a not altogether exciting syllabus. The highest form were 'reading Euripides, the Greek Testament, Virgil, Salust etc and are doing Euclid and Algebra....' The rest of the boys were studying 'English and English History, English Themes and French'. The results of the Arithmetic lessons 'bore testimony to the good behaviour of the boys'.

By January 1857, Mr Twells was looking out for Drawing and French masters and also to have the school lit by gas as soon as a 'main' was brought to the house. Meantime, he sought a refund for the lighting of the school by candles. April '57 saw 70 pupils in attendance and 15 turned down through lack of space. The good behaviour seemed to be slipping too as Mr Twells reported that four boys had been expelled, having been found guilty of 'theft and being otherwise hurtful to the tone of the school'.

Expenses were already rising; the cost of cleaning the School had increased from 1s 6d to 2s (7p to 10p). But income had risen too, and somehow, by 1858, they were fitting 106 boys into the now cramped schoolrooms, where the three teachers were struggling to cope as still more arrived. By 1859 there were an amazing 120 'Dolphins'.

Map of the 'hamlet' of Hammersmith

Encouraged by the energetic and persevering Mr Twells, the Trustees decided that they needed larger premises. A Mr Scott had 'three acres, 2 rods and 22 poles of land for sale at £800 to the north of the newly built St John's Church, close to Hammersmith Grove'. The Trustees inspected the site and found it 'well drained but full of couch grass'. A gardener was ordered to clear the land and, by some confusion of tasks, a 'navigator' – a navvy – who had been working on the new railway was also asked to do the work, and had to be paid, although neither seems to have been successful. Eventually, the land was let, rent-free, to a 'respectable' local market gardener 'who has forked, cleansed and planted it with potatoes and agreed to give it up clean, level and fit for planting with grass seed by January 1860'. (£10 was set aside for this, to include the grass seed and for 'advance planning'.)

At the same time, it was agreed to offer a prize of £10 to the architect who provided the best plans for a new school. Even in those days, it was not a great amount but, nevertheless, four were submitted under pseudonyms to ensure impartial judging. From plans marked 'Vobiscum', 'Quid dem', 'Cavendo Tutus' and 'Faith', the Trustees chose the plan marked 'Faith'. The envelope was opened and the name of the architect emerged: Mr Charles H Cooke of 11 John Street, Bedford Row, London. The cost of the new building in Victorian Gothic style was agreed at £5,875. Predictably, within two years the cost had risen to more than £7,000 but there was no turning back. The building work had started and the Trustees were forced to take out a mortgage.

Crinolines and countryside – architect Charles Cooke's impression of the new Godolphin School, 1861 (From *The Builder* 1861)

7

The school magazine, *The Dolphin*, described the scene on Saturday, 8 June 1861, as 'a day that will long be remembered with pleasure by all the present Godolphin boys ... the laying of the First Stone of that building which, when completed, will be an honour to Hammersmith.

'In the morning a friendly game at cricket took place on Shepherd's Bush between past and present members of the School. (Taking all the good play of our opponents into consideration, it must be admitted by all that when a whole Eleven makes but four runs off the bat it deserves some censure.)'

There was only time for one innings before 'all late pupils and scholars met at the present building to proceed to the new site at Bradmore, near St John's Church, to witness the ceremony of the Day.

'About three o'clock ... a procession was formed consisting of the present scholars, the Rev H Twells, the Rev T B Hill and other masters, late pupils, Trustees and the Bishop and clergy of the neighbourhood. The bells of the Parish church merrily rang out a peal and though the sun did not shine on us, yet the threatening rain did not descend.

'The arrangements on the ground were very good. In front of the Bishop's chair a large platform was erected for visitors whilst on the other side of him, the Trustees and clergy and the scholars were placed. It cannot be said that there was any lack of spectators. Upwards of 1,000 were seated on the large platform alone...'

The Bishop of London, Dr Archibald Campbell Tait, laid the foundation stone, Lord Ebury, Chairman of the Trustees, whose hard work and determination had brought the Godolphin Charity back to life, made a speech and expressed pleasure at the presence of two ladies. The magazine described the stone, which bore the inscription:

This stone
was laid by
The Lord Bishop of London
June 8th, 1861

Charles H. Cooke, Architect.

It noted also 'some hieroglyphics' in each corner which were the initials of the Headmaster, the visitors of the School, the Dean of St Paul's and the Dean of Westminster, the Godolphin heirs and the architect.

The report added, as an aside, 'It may, perhaps, be mentioned here that in a cavity of the stone a bottle was placed in which were enclosed the first two numbers of the Magazine'.

The Bishop's speech contained some remarkable words. He had, he explained, often been called upon to lay the first stones of schools for the poorer classes, but this was a school of another description and yet equally important. 'If the middle and upper classes do not look to it that their sons are properly instructed, they will soon find that those of a lower grade are fast treading on their heels', he warned. 'This is an age of progress; the standard of education in the national schools has been materially raised, and surely the schools for the higher ranks of society should be properly elevated'. Turning to the boys, 'he entreated them to look after themselves or they would find the boys of the national schools tread on their heels; and especially to be particular in conduct because they might have a good school house and good school masters but all would be unavailing unless they had a proper tone among themselves'.

With a passing thought that 'the youth of to-day were in danger of being examined to death although the boys of the School... had worthily passed the ordeal', he hoped 'that God would send down his blessings on this work, done in his faith and fear'.

The ceremony was followed by a giant tea party and the date was set aside for perpetuity as Founders' Day.

Later, the magazine described the new school:

'As you stand on the north side of St John's Church and look towards the front of the building, the projecting part on the right, with its large window, is the south end of the Schoolroom (which is) 93 ft long by 25 ft broad, thus contains 2,325 square feet. (Our present schoolroom in Great Church Lane contains about 1,140 square feet and is thus not half the size of that in the new building). The shape of the new schoolroom is purposely arranged in order that the boys may be on one side, in parallel desks, and the masters on the other. The entrance to the schoolroom will be by the porch at the north end. Beneath the large north window there will be a covered shed for play and etc in wet weather.

The four windows on the ground floor to the left of the schoolroom... are the windows of two rooms to be used, during school time, as classrooms and, out of School, as sitting rooms for the upper and lower boarders.

Next is a private study of the master in charge of boarders. Then comes the main entrance, which is to be paved with encaustic tiles and from which will proceed a stone staircase, leading up to the dormitories. The three windows on the left of the main entrance are those of the dining hall, capable of accommodating from 40–50 boys. Still further to the left is the large window of the Head Master's dining room. We then have an ornamental porch leading to the Head Master's house. To the extreme left is the drawing room and behind it the library. The kitchen, housekeeper's apartment, etc are at the back.

The line of the windows above the main part of the ground floor belong to the dormitories, with the exception of the oriel window which is the bedroom of the master in charge. The range of windows at the top of the house belong to the servants' rooms, sick room, etc...'

In front of the building was to be a private drive and the ground between the school and the churchyard was to be laid out, as it is to this day, with turf and shrubs and behind, a gravel playground and beyond it, a cricket field.

The boys entered the new school, briefly, for the first time on Prize Day 1862, and the new half year began on 5 August 1862. The fees were raised from £6 to £8, but costs continued to increase as Mr Twells sought more and more essential equipment, and although Hammersmith Parish Council reduced the rates from £280 to £190, the fees had reached £10 a year by 1865.

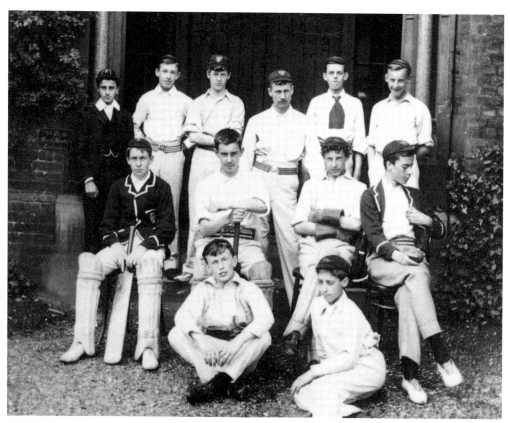

A Godolphin School cricket team, 1894 (Courtesy Hammersmith and Fulham Archives and Local History Collection)

From then, 'this wonder of Hammersmith' progressed steadily if not spectacularly. The Godolphin book, issued to every boy on entering the school, shows that the uniform was a black coat and waistcoat (and, presumably, black striped trousers), and a clean and tidy appearance was to be maintained both in morning and afternoon school. All boys wore the school cap, which had a single dolphin badge above the peak. This cost 2s (10p). Before new caps could be bought, the old one had to be handed in 'to prevent them from being obtained by street boys'. 'Street boys' seem to have been a thorn in the flesh. Rule 11 makes clear that 'stone-throwing, the possession of cata-pults, fireworks, matches and the like, snowballs (except in the field) and any intercourse or quarrel with street boys and also playing in the streets will be severely punished'.

Although there had been no buildings – only fields – round the school when it was built, Hammersmith was growing rapidly. Houses were built in Cambridge Grove on one side and Oxford (later Iffley) Road on the other and, in 1867, not without some problems over the destination of hard-hit cricket balls, a factory was built at the top of Cambridge Grove. However, the Godolphin School was evidently failing to keep pace with the growth. Trustees had other interests and often failed to attend meetings. The once glowing reports from outside examiners began to suggest that all was not well with the standards of learning. In 1870, despite all his efforts, Henry Twells gave up, resigned and went to become a country rector. His successor lasted barely three years before sending in his letter of resignation, which said, bluntly, 'I have done what I could to keep up the School, but with indifferent success and I believe that the only chance of its regaining its former position lies in a change of management...'

Briefly, admissions increased to a peak in 1891 when there were 200 boys, but despite the appointment of more trustees – mostly local churchmen – the downward trend continued until finally disaster struck. There was apprehension when St Paul's, one of the country's oldest and most famous public schools, moved from the City to Hammersmith Road in 1882, and gloom when, in 1895, Latymer Upper School opened in King Street.

Probably the most famous and illustrious Dolphin boy was the poet and playwright W B Yeats, who was not an altogether happy pupil. In his bio-graphy of Yeats, (*W B Yeats, 1865–1939*, Macmillan, 1942) Joseph Hone sug-gests that this was 'a school for the sons of struggling professional men' which Yeats, in his autobiography, had described as 'rough' and 'cheap'. He was there from 1875–1880, when his parents were living in West Kensington, and in 1911 still preserved several of his school reports and a timetable of lessons, drawn up by himself, in which he noted 'Scripter', 'Riting', 'Reading', 'Inglish', 'Gramar' and 'Arithmithic'. Hone explains – unnecessa-rily perhaps – that Yeats' spelling was always bad and to the end of his days he wrote 'exhausted' as 'exausted'. His best subject was Latin, where he was eighth in a class of 31. His Conduct was 'very good', his Mathematics 'very poor' and his French *'faible, sans énergie'*. In his book *Reveries*, Yeats recalls: 'I had a harassed life and got many a black eye and had many outbursts of grief and rage... I was ashamed of my lack of courage'.

'Willie' Yeats was remembered as a gentle boy, with little physical strength but one who 'tries to do as well as he can'. In his last term, however, he did win a silver cup in a running race.

Despite his later fame, his name fails to appear in the *Gloria Domus* of the School, which lists, among other more acceptable former pupils, Sir F H

Laking, Surgeon Apothecary to Queen Victoria, and Sir Leander Starr Jameson, who gave his name to a disastrous raid which preceded the Boer War and who, later, became Premier of South Africa. A plaque commemorating Jameson's life still survives in the School.

GODOLPHIN SCHOOL, HAMMERSMITH.

HALF-YEARLY REPORT

Of Conduct and Progress.

Lent Term, 1877

NAME.	FORM.	Place in Form of 31 Boys, by				
		Classics.	Mathematics.	Mod. Languages.	English.	Total Marks.
Yeats	I	6	27	18.	19	1197 21

GENERAL WORK.

Only fair. Perhaps better in Latin than in any other subject. Very poor in spelling

L. T. Morris. *Form Master.*

MATHEMATICS.

Moderate only. Works carefully, but is slow.

L. T. Morris.

MODERN LANGUAGES.

pretty good

Barret

HOLIDAY TASK. *Revision of History & Geography done during Term.*

Rupert H Morris *Head Master.*

The School re-opens Tuesday, April 17th at 9 A.M., when all Boys are *absolutely* required to be present.

William Butler Yeats's Godolphin School Report, 1877

In 1897 the Trustees were replaced by a Governing Body which consisted of a representative of the London County Council (which had taken over from the old Metropolitan Board of Works in 1888); one from Middlesex County Council; one put forward by the Bishop of London and the Deans of St Paul's and Westminster; and one 'by the Council of University College until the Institution of a Teaching University for London and then by such University'. There would be other members, including one to represent the Godolphin family.

It was all too late. Numbers were falling as more pupils left. By December 1900 the Godolphin School for Boys had finally closed its doors and the new Governors, in debt and despair, were making plans to demolish the building and sell the land for housing development.

3

INTERREGNUM

Fortunes may have been at a low ebb, but for the School founded on the plan called 'Faith', spring 1901 brought a glimmer of hope – and charity.

On 15 February of that year, at a meeting in London, the Chief Charity Commissioner suggested to the Governors of Latymer Upper that some of the wealthy Latymer Endowment should be applied to founding a girls' school.

Edward Latymer, a sixteenth-century feltmaker, had made a fortune in his service to Queen Elizabeth I and as Clerk of the Court of Wards and Liveries in the City of London. He seems to have been an amiable character, cheerful, religious, charitable and sociable, and he left £2,500 of his wealth to his friends. (This included his gilt and silver bowls, canary cups, damask napkins, turkey-work chairs, linen, ruffs and his 'little silk purse' as well as his gold ring set with diamonds.) But the greater part of his money went to help the poor and needy, particularly in the foundation of educational trusts.

One of these trusts was committed to founding schools for poor boys in two areas where he owned land, one in Edmonton, north of London, and another which paid for eight poor boys between the ages of eight and twelve in Hammersmith, who were to be clothed and 'put to some petty school' to learn to read English until they attained the age of thirteen, at which point they were to be 'instructed in some part of God's religion'.

In Hammersmith, the money was used to pay for boys to go to other charity schools until 1756, when a schoolhouse was built for them near what is now Hammersmith Broadway. By 1816 the number of Latymer Foundation boys had increased to 30 and some girls were taught also, under the Latymer Female Charity (later to become part of the Latymer and Hammersmith Charity). Not all of them were as demure as might be expected, and the Minutes of the meetings of Trustees mention girls being punished for 'saucy behaviour'. In 1821 they led the funeral procession for Queen Caroline, walking in a group with Latymer boys.

By the 1840s the Female Charity School was linked with St Paul's Church and had 50 girls on its register. They appear to have been taught to read and write, as well as helping to support the School with needlework and other useful skills learnt for their 'careers', mostly as servants.

Details from the Minute books show that one of the tasks of the brighter

Latymer charity boys and girls lead Queen Caroline's funeral procession – 1821

girls was to copy the School accounts, and a page, dated 1845, detailing the cost of their summer and winter uniforms, has a note at the end: 'Copied by J. Burgis Aged 13 yrs'.

Expenses included '360 yards Blue Camlet for Frocks, Coats and Tippets' costing £23 5s (£23.25); 137½ yards of dowlas (a coarse linen cloth) for shifts totalling £6 17s 6d (£6.87); 50 straw bonnets – £4 7s 6d (£4.37); and 50 pairs of shoes – £10 16s 8d (£10.32). Even the 50 haircuts were listed.

As the nineteenth century progressed, London expanded rapidly, and by the 1890s, Edward Latymer's original fields and market gardens were in brisk demand for housing development, factories and the expanding railway services. (The Metropolitan Line had reached Hammersmith in 1864, the London & South Western Railway trains began running in a loop from Waterloo round Shepherds Bush towards Richmond in 1869 and the District Line station at the Broadway was opened in 1874.) These, as well as horse-drawn buses and, later, trams, were reaching out to what were, by now, thriving suburbs. Sale of part of this land had swelled the funds of the Foundation and it was from this money, said the Charity Commissioners, that some provision should be made for girls' education.

To comply with this demand, Latymer Governors had, for some time, been looking for suitable premises for such a school. The Godolphin building seemed to offer a heaven-sent answer to their problem.

The February meeting in 1901 was attended by General Goldsworthy, Admiral Hardy and Mr Charles Wigan, Clerk to the Godolphin School (who, with his son who succeeded him, gave years of loyal service to Godolphin and Latymer) and the Mayor of Hammersmith, Mr Chamberlen (in whose memory the school organ was built). After inspecting the Iffley Road buildings and examining all the financial and legal details, Mr Chamberlen promised, on behalf of the Latymer Foundation, that the Latymer Trustees would co-operate with the Godolphin Trustees in endowing a girls' school.

In the event, Latymer paid off the outstanding mortgage on the Iffley Road building, contributed £8,000 towards the cost of converting it into a school for girls and granted a further £500 a year towards its upkeep. (The £500 is still being paid.) On 2 May, 1902 the new scheme for a girls' school was signed by General Goldsworthy, Sir William Wills (later to become

15

Female Charity School.

			£	s.	d.
AMOUNT BROUGHT OVER	- - - - -		52	18	5
360 Yards of Blue Camlet, for Frocks, Coats, and Tippets,	at	1/3½	23	5	"
104 Yards of Flannel - - - - - - -	at	1/-	5	4	"
137½ Yards of Dowlas for Shifts - - - - - -	at	1/-	6	17	6
82 Yards of Irish for Aprons and Tippets - - - -	at	1/11½	8	-	7
82½ Yards of Check for Pinafores - - - - -	at	1/-	4	2	6
48 Yards of Cotton for Linings - - - - -	at	-	"	16	"
12 Yards of Muslin for Caps - - - - - -	at	-	"	16	6
Yards of Riband for Bonnets and Caps - - - -	at				
Thread, Tape, Binding, Buttons, &c. - - - -	-		3	1	7½
50 Straw Bonnets - - - - - - -	at	1/9	4	7	6
50 Pair of Stays - - - - - - -	at	2/3	5	12	6
50 Pair of Shoes - - - - - - -	at	4/4	10	16	8
50 Pair of Black Worsted Stockings - - - -	at	1/-	2	10	"
125 Yards of Dowlas for Shifts - - - - -	at	1/-	6	5	"
Yards of Irish for Aprons and Tippets - - - -	at				
70 Yards of Check for Pinafores - - - - -	at	1/1½	3	7	"
Yards of Flannel - - - - - - -	at				
50 Pair of Stockings - - - - - - -	at	1/-	2	10	"
50 Pair of Shoes - - - - - - -	at	4/4	10	16	8
Thread, Tape, Needles, &c. - - - - -					
Yards of Grey Bath Coating for Cloaks - - -	at				
Lackering the Badges - - - - - -	at				
Ditto, New - - - - - - - -	at				
50 Pair of Stockings - - - - - - -	at	1/0½	2	3	9
50 Pair of Shoes - - - - - - -	at	4/4	10	16	8
Linen for Towels and Bags - - - - -	at				
S. Abrahart, attending Girls St. Peters			2	15	
Teachers, on leaving School — — —			1	8	4
J. C. Read, Painter — — —			6	11	10
G. Bennett, Hair Cutting — — —			1	11	3
C. Millwood, Bricklayer &c. —			3	19	6
J. Gomme, Carpenter — — —			4	3	2
R. Bland, Carpenter — — —				2	3
Jas. Whale, Posting Sermon Bills				7	6
Stamps — — —				1	9
Mr. Jas. Bird, Solicitor — — —			16	6	2

Row labels (bracketed in left margin): Lady Day., Michaelmas., Christmas., EXTRAS.

Copied by
J. Burges Aged 12 years.

TOTAL - - - £ | 201 | 15 | 10½

Uniform list for the Latymer and Hammersmith Charity Females, circa 1840
(Courtesy, Latymer Upper School)

Lord Winterstoke, in whose memory the Winterstoke Scholarships are named) and Mr A Hubbard. In this, it was stipulated that the name Godolphin should take precedence over that of Latymer. When the final scheme was drawn up on 23 December 1903, there was also a provision that £4,000 should be paid to the Godolphin School, Salisbury to provide them with a new playing-field.

Miss Gertrude Clement, B.A.

New Governors took over and appointed Miss Gertrude Clement as their first Head Mistress. Her qualifications included a B.A. from the Royal Holloway College, London University; Oxford Honour School of English Language and Literature; and Distinction in the Oxford Teachers' Diploma. She had already been Assistant Mistress of Bradford Grammar School and Head of Stamford High School. She chose nine assistant teachers, plus a Drawing teacher, two for Class Singing and Pianoforte and one for Swedish Drill ('Certificated by Madame Bergman Osterberg'.)

Miss Clement and staff – 1907

4

A SCHOOL OF DOLPHINS

There can be no better description of the new Head Mistress than that given in an earlier history of the School by her own pupils:

'The strength of [her] personality is attested by the remarkable consistency of the impression retained by those who attended the School in its earliest days. She laid, well and truly, the foundations of our School traditions, but also, in no less a degree, established principles of conduct in the individuals with whom she had to deal . . .'

'Her character was evident in her cool and graceful bearing – her quiet dignified movement'.

'Miss Clement was never flustered and never raised her voice. She was a perfect example of deportment'.

'It was her large, dark brown, penetrating eyes which made her face remarkable: the eyes that danced, laughed and sparkled when she was amused, which seemed to grow even larger when she was interested, but which, alas for sinners, darkened, glinted and penetrated your very soul when she was angry'.

'I dreaded being sent to her for running in the corridor'.

Her style as a speaker was described as concise, forceful, impressive and at times scathing: 'Looking back on Speech Days I have the impression that she felt she must make the most of her chance to drive home the great importance of education, besides performing the very gratifying duty of announcing the ever growing list of successes won by her beloved school. . . . My father, a barrister of her own generation, had the highest opinion of her intellectual powers and said that the clearness and vigour of her mind were on a par with those of some of the finest High Court judges'.

Her thorough knowledge of the School and all its members was remarked again and again: 'By the end of the first term, Miss Clement could say once more that she knew every one of the five hundred girls'. At her weekly mark readings her comments were often embarrassingly individual and more than one Old Dolphin recalling the 'extraordinary awe and respect' in which she was held, remembers too 'the way in which she knew everything about us, however little we saw of her personally'.

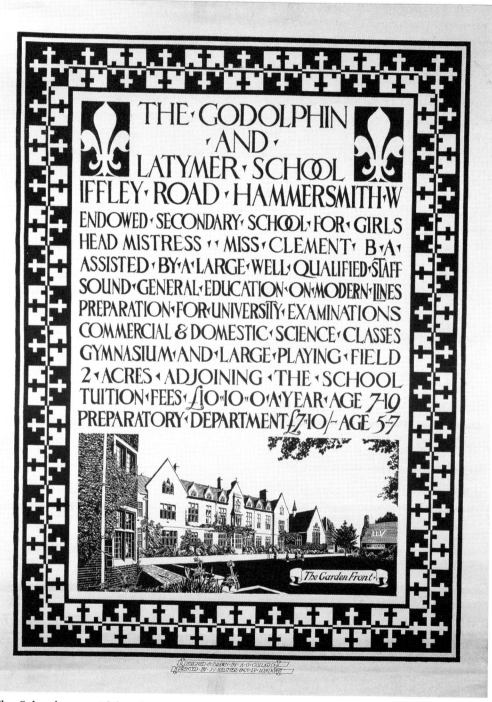

The School was widely advertised . . .

By her own discipline – her personality and magnetism – she inculcated pride in and loyalty to the School. She had an eagle eye for mannerless behaviour but she also taught the more difficult virtues of leadership. 'She continually instilled into our minds the thought that we must be prepared to accept responsibility. This, together with self-control and self-discipline, love of fair play and justice and the readiness to help others, were the precepts of conduct...'

The building in Iffley Road was still undergoing massive alterations so the new Godolphin and Latymer School for Girls started life, like its masculine predecessor, in temporary premises, which this time had been known as Hammersmith High School, at 251 King Street. Advertisements appeared in local papers and in Hammersmith underground stations, and on 4 May 1905 the first girls arrived – later to take on the proud nickname of 'the Aborigines' – the founding members of this School of Dolphins. In December 1905, 13 of them were entered for the Cambridge Local Examination and 11 passed.

By January 1906 the building was ready

By January 1906 the renovated school was ready, complete with a new Head Mistress's house and a schoolkeeper's lodge at the gates through which Miss Clement led her new scholars. The building was formally reopened by the Duke of Leeds (from Leeds Castle in Kent – a relative by marriage of the Godolphin family) on 1 March 1906. (A plaque commemorating this hangs in the cloisters.)

The eagle emblem of the Godolphin family was combined with the Latymer crosses to form the School badge, but the girls' retained the Godolphin motto *Francha leale toge* and the nickname – 'Dolphins' – which has stayed with them ever since. The School colours were red and white.

Godolphin and Latymer opened at a crucial time for girls' education. For half a century a band of intelligent women had been rebelling against the idea that females were inferior to males in every way and needed no useful training in anything outside home and social life. As long ago as 1864, a Schools Inquiry Commission (chaired by Lord Taunton) had been appointed to look into the whole question of secondary education for girls as well as boys. Among the pioneers who gave evidence were the redoubtable Miss Frances Mary Buss and Miss Dorothea Beale, both determined head mistresses, Miss Buss at North London Collegiate School and Miss Beale at Cheltenham Ladies' College. They were, inevitably, butts of contemporary humour and targets of the famous rhyme:

> Miss Buss and Miss Beale
> Cupid's darts do not feel;
> They are not like us
> Miss Beale and Miss Buss.

Also there, putting the case for girls' education, was at least one sympathetic male. James Bryce, an assistant commissioner at the time, wrote in the Report: 'Although the world has now existed for several thousand years, the notion that women have minds as cultivable and worth cultivating as men's minds is still regarded by the ordinary British parent as an offensive, not to say a revolutionary, paradox'.

Aspirations were lofty. *Work and Play for Girls' Schools*, published in 1889, pleaded:

> Tis life, not death, for which we pant
> More life and fuller that we want.

The head mistresses, particularly, had a passion for educational excellence, striving 'to counteract what is low and base and to cultivate all that is true and lovely'.

These were the initial skirmishes, but as the nineteenth century went on, the battling pioneers came together in 1874 to found the Association of Head Mistresses and consolidate their campaign. Gradually the idea of educating, first, middle- and upper-class girls whose parents could afford to pay fees at private schools and then all girls, whatever their home circumstances, began to gain ground. Already, under the great Education Act of 1870, School Boards had been set up to provide free elementary education for (mostly) working-class children to the age of 11 or 12. Now, under the 1902 Education Act, this was to be extended to include secondary schools.

Higher education for women was beginning to take shape too, and between 1869 – when Girton College was founded – and 1900, a succession of colleges, including Newnham, Newcastle College of Science, Somerville, Lady Margaret Hall, St Hugh's, Westfield and the Royal Holloway College, all opened their doors to women, although the universities were not yet ready to grant them degrees (and for Cambridge, this was delayed until after World War II).

In the early 1900s the London County Council not only built a number of secondary schools for girls but helped other fee-paying academic schools with grants, on condition that they accepted a proportion of bright youngsters who had passed the scholarship examinations which were held at eleven plus in the elementary schools. Godolphin was one of the independent schools which, from the beginning, welcomed scholarship girls and, indeed, offered some scholarships of its own.

For the struggling women schoolteachers, these were heady days, and the young Miss Clement must have felt that 24 hours was too short to cope with everything that had to be done.

Established in her new house (where the Music Department stands now) she set about the task of making the School a success. In the first prospectus, a small square booklet with the name of the School and the new badge in blue on its cover, she outlined for parents the opportunities which Godolphin and Latymer could offer their daughters:

The Head Mistress's House

23

The hall had been the boys' schoolroom

The new buildings had 12 large classrooms, an assembly hall, library, a cookery room, a gymnasium 'equipped with all the necessary apparatus for Swedish drill', the fashionable equivalent of the eurhythmics of the 1990s, and three Science laboratories (for Chemistry, Physics and Botany) 'fitted up with all modern requirements'.

Reports of Governors' meetings and Miss Clement's own notebook testify to the amount of pressure which she put on them to make sure that every-

Botanical laboratories . . .

thing which went into the School was of the highest standard, and one can't help feeling that they must have dreaded the moment when she presented yet another 'shopping list'. As early as 1904 they had provided 100 single desks, 6

... and botanical garden

Miss Clement's penetrating eye missed nothing – 1907

mistresses' desks, 6 platforms, 6 blackboards, a piano (price limit £50) and 100 chairs. Now there was a call for more desks and chairs, books, maps, scientific equipment plus a horse-drawn mower to keep the playing field in shape – and staff to use it. Miss Clement checked everything meticulously – even the coal merchants who provided fuel for the school's open fires in every classroom and the window cleaners – came under her scrutiny, and if their service was not approved, their contracts were ended and more efficient suppliers sought.

The prospectus assured parents that 'much care and attention have been given to the choice of the School furniture. In the Upper School, desks have been used which can be adjusted to the different height and size of the pupils. Ground glass blackboards have been fixed in all the large class-rooms and a special preparation of black cement to cover the walls of the art room gives ample scope for practice in "free-arm" drawing'.

'Free arm drawing' in the first Art room

Added to these attractions was 'perhaps the richest possession ... the playing field on the School premises ... the lungs of Hammersmith ... where the girls may enjoy hockey, tennis, basketball, cricket and other games and they will have every opportunity of developing physically'.

Fees had been fixed at 10 guineas (£10.50) a year, together with a small extra charge for stationery. The curriculum included 'all subjects generally taught in secondary schools, the work being carried to University standard'. Exceptional opportunities were promised for learning Science, with Botany studied on 'a large piece of ground which has been set aside for a botanical garden'.

For those who might not be able to afford full fees, there were not only

Netball on 'the lungs of Hammersmith'

the LCC Junior County Scholarships but Governors' Scholarships, reserved for girls at 'public elementary schools' within Hammersmith at the rate of one to every 20 Dolphins. These could be supplemented by a grant of £10 a year for those in special need, plus a similar number of Foundation Scholarships. Exhibitions of £25 and £50 a year were tenable for three years at any university.

'Domestic Science is taught'

The restored building had space for 310 pupils but by October 1906 there were already 328 registered. Miss Clement asked for the limit to be raised to 500 and even offered to give up her Head Mistress's house to accommodate a further 70 girls (and, at the same time, save the Inhabited House Duty of the period), but the offer was refused.

Interestingly, none of the staff – teachers or maintenance – was insured and it was not until 1907 that the Governors began to consider taking out policies to cover them. Money was already disappearing fast as teaching salaries were raised to a maximum of £200 a year, but they decided that insurance was essential and acted accordingly.

'The School is thriving' – 1907

There was little doubt that the School was thriving although the cash flow was always slim. By April 1907 there were 367 girls attending, of whom 78 were LCC scholars, and the Governors were turning their minds to holidays – for Ascension Day, Empire Day and Foundation Day. They agreed on Ascension Day (all day) and Foundation Day, on which the annual Sports Day would also be held, but not Empire Day, although they recommended that there should be 'some patriotic or loyal demonstration or address to call special attention to the day. This might take the form of the erection of a flagstaff'. Now, too, for the first time, parents were asked to help with voluntary contributions towards the cost of school prizes (a request which met with an enthusiastic response and continued until it was taken over and funded by the PTA, who still contribute towards the cost of prizes).

Sports Day for charity . . .

Summer 1907 saw the first gymnastic display in connection with the Mayor of Hammersmith's Cripple Children's Fund and a Sports Day with refreshments served on the field. There were refreshments, too, at ninepence (approx 3p) per head for the 300 guests at Speech Day that year – a grand

. . . elegantly supervised

occasion when the *Hymnus Godolphianus* was sung by the girls for the first time. The hymn had been written for the boys' school in 1876 by the Second Master, the Rev. J A Evans, who explained: 'In form, it is an imitation of the

29

Energetic races for everyone ...

... but who won?

'The wheel' demanded concentration

rhymed hymns of mediaeval monkish Latin and in substance, a paraphrase of vv 1, 2, 11, 12 and 15 of Psalm 144', and was used as a proper psalm for Founder's Day in 1877.

The words read:

> *Sit benedictus Dominus*
> *Qui docet nos pugnare,*
> *In dextra pollens gladius*
> *Hostes exsuperare.*
>
> *Spes et castellum validum*
> *Arx hominum servatrix;*
> *Bellando scutum ferreum*
> *Virtus opitulatrix.*
>
> *Defende nobis iuvenes*
> *Malos, Deus benigne,*
> *Crementur falsae imagines*
> *In veritatis igne.*
>
> *Sic erunt nostrae filiae*
> *Flores tuis in hortis*
> *Et posthac stabunt candidi*
> *Postes in templi portis.*
>
> *Quam felix iste populus*
> *Qui tali gaudet fato*
> *Sic benedictas Dominus*
> *Nos semper adiuvato.*
>
> Amen

This was translated as:

> All praise and worship be to Thee,
> Who teacheth us the way to fight,
> A mighty brand in God's right hand,
> To strike down every enemy.
>
> Thou art our hope, and Thou indeed
> Our fortress of salvation sure;
> An iron shield in open field,
> Our succour in the hour of need.

31

Defend us from the snares of youth
O God of Love, and keep us pure,
Let all false phantasy of man
Perish in Thy consuming truth.

Oh may all these within Thy walls
So grow as plants beneath Thy care,
That they hereafter may appear
As polished pillars in Thy Halls.

Thrice happy they – and only they –
Who live rejoicing in Thy strength,
O God, defend this school and send
Thy blessing down on us alway.

                                    Amen

In 1994 a later translation of the Godolphin Hymn was used at Dame Joyce
Bishop's Memorial Service in St Margaret's Church, Westminster.

Blessings upon the Lord our God
Who teaches us how we must fight:
A mighty sword to take in hand
To overcome the foes of Right.

For hope he gives, as a strong fort,
A citadel that saves mankind;
In field of war an iron shield –
Courage that grows with strength of mind.

Deliver us, good Lord our God,
From joys that bring but grief and shame;
Let lying fantasy be scorched
In testing truth's consuming flame.

So shall our generation be
Fair flowers in your garden, Lord;
And evermore stand shining bright
As pillars at your temple's court.

How happy is that nation then
Which destiny meets unafraid;
Thus blessed, may the blessed Lord
Be there at hand to give us aid.

No uniform for the 'aborigines'

There was no School uniform – girls wore the accepted long skirts and long-sleeved blouses of the late Edwardians and early Georgians. Contemporary photographs show them at work with serious dedication in the classrooms and on the playing-field. However, the Head's reports suggest that they might not all have been such paragons. In 1907 she suspended and later threatened to expel one early pupil for, among other things, 'unbecoming conduct with the Ravenscourt Park Station Master'. One can only imagine her indignation at this behaviour, made worse when she was threatened with legal action for 'slanderous statements' by the equally indignant Station Master.

Music, singing and drama played a major part in the School life from its inception, and another early Prize Day included not only the School Hymn but a 'Pianoforte Quartctt' (sic) by N Bush, A Best, E Galton and F Flexman playing the Grand March from Wagner's *Tannhäuser*; Forms Lower II, II and I in an action song, *Simple Simon*; Forms Lower IV, Remove and Upper IIA singing *Golden Slumbers* and *O No John*, followed by the Upper School singing a part-song, *The Nights* by Roberti. A pianoforte solo *L'Harmonie des Anges* by Burgmuller, played by D Evans, was followed by another roll-icking action song, 'words by Miss Armfield, music by Mrs Watson' – *The Song of the Playing Field*.

Drama flourished – *Masque of May Morning* was one of the first plays

Staff joined in this early *Merchant of Venice*

King Catarrho – 1911

VIth form and prefects – 1911

This was the heyday of the suffragette movement, demanding votes for women and at least slightly more equality with men, but it still comes as something of a shock to think of these apparently demure young women chorusing:

> All boys, we're told, in a bygone day
> Said 'Girls are stupid, they cannot play.
> They cannot run, they cannot throw'.
> We've changed all that as we mean to show.

(Chorus) 'Play up then girls, play up, play up!
> Tomorrow you'll win if you fail to-day.
> An uphill fight in a losing game
> Will show the boys that girls can play.

> For this is the way we hold a bat,
> When it's time to bowl, we bowl like that,
> We'll show you the way to catch a ball,
> We field, keep wicket, yes, one and all.

'The underhand service, skimming low' – tennis champions.

Lawn tennis we play, and well we know
The underhand service skimming low,
The overhand cut that shoots a yard,
The backhand twister that comes in hard.

In hockey you'll find it's just the same
Whatever we do, we play the game,
We'll dribble the ball a whole field's length
Or shoot a goal with a well-judged strength.

'We'll dribble a ball ...! School hockey team – 1911

We've several teams for a net-ball match,
Good throwers-in and girls who can catch,
For every game we've a golden rule,
Don't play for self but play for the School.

The Order of Proceedings shows that speeches were made by the Chairman of Governors, Thomas Chamberlen Esq, JP; The Duke of Leeds, the Bishop of Worcester, Lord Winterstoke of Blagdon, Sir William Bull (MP for Hammersmith), Miss Roberts (Head Mistress of Bradford Grammar School) and Miss Clement.

These were followed by an assortment of music, including a song which, no doubt, accurately reflected the feelings of that time. Under the title *There's a Land*, it went:

There's a land, a dear land, where the rights of the free
Though firm as the earth, are as wide as the sea;
Where the primroses bloom, and the nightingales sing,
And the honest, poor man is as good as a king.

(*Chorus*) Show'ry! Flow'ry!!
Cheerful! Tearful!
England, wave guarded, and green to the shore!
West-land! Best-land!
Thy land! My land!
Glory be with her, and Peace evermore!

There's a land, a dear land, where our vigour of soul
Is fed by the tempests that blow from the Pole;
Where people love Peace, but at sound of the drum
A myriad of soldiers and heroes become.

(*Chorus*) Sea-land! Free land!
Fairest! Rarest!
Home of brave men and the girls they adore.
Fearless! Peerless!
Thy land! My land!
Glory be with her, and Peace evermore!

The old gymnasium adjoining the Science laboratories had been the boys' chapel

Sadly, there was to be no 'peace evermore'. Within the next decade, many of the girls who sang so hopefully of peace and happiness were, with their 'fearless, peerless' sweethearts and husbands, to be plunged into the First World War, emerging at the end as spinsters or widows for the rest of their lives.

For the time being, life was good.

Action inside the old gymnasium

Civil Service 'A' – 1911

The Board of Education held its first full inspection in February 1909 and reported that there were 404 day pupils (which rapidly increased to more than 500) including 100 scholarship holders in 18 forms starting with eight-year-olds and continuing through to eighteen-year-olds. Of these, 35 per cent came from public elementary schools and 30 per cent were scholarship holders. There were also ten bursary holders and five student teachers. The greatest number of pupils – 246 – came from Hammersmith.

Perhaps, to those reading it 90 years later, one of the most surprising sections of the Inspectors' Report, and one which reflected the importance of social status in Britain at the period in which it was written, was headed *Class in Life and Area from which drawn*:

CLASS:	No. of Pupils
Professional, Independent etc.	114
Merchants, Manufacturers etc	39
Retail Traders.	76
Farmers★	3
Commercial Managers.	106
Service (domestic & other) Postmen etc. Artisans	66

(★There were still many farms within walking distance of Iffley Road, including those in Barnes, where there were also market gardens.)

Unlike the Boys' School, there was no heavy emphasis on religious teaching and learning the Catechism. Religious teaching was, from the beginning, non-denominational and, said the Inspectors, very few girls took advantage of the Conscience Clause which allowed their withdrawal from it. For the most part, the subjects were considered to be taught well – with increasing efficiency as the School, which was rapidly becoming overcrowded, moved into the new extensions. Needlework seems to have been one of the less illustrious areas, and the Report suggested that patterns followed might include 'a shoe bag, "cottage" pinafore, simple bath wrap (in the "Flannel Grade"), child's calico knickers, overalls, nightgowns, skirt and circular bands and a bodice group'.

But the overall Report was glowing: 'The School is fortunate in the possession of a Head Mistress of remarkable ability and intellectual force', they said. 'The gratifying development and success are in a large measure due to her energy, thought and administrative power.... It has made an excellent beginning and has justified its existence in a most striking manner ... it has already shown that it met an urgent need in Hammersmith and in the educational scheme of London ... and it should have a distinguished career of usefulness before it'.

On the crest of the wave, Miss Clement surged ahead and by 1913 was

Do come and bring your friends.

The Godolphin and Latymer School,

IFFLEY ROAD, HAMMERSMITH, W.

═══════════

A CHRISTMAS BAZAAR

will be held in the School Hall on

December 18 and 19, from 3.30 to 10 p.m.,

and on

December 20, from 3—9 p.m.

The object of the Bazaar is to raise money to provide an organ for the school.

The Bazaar will be opened on Thursday, December 18, by

LADY BULL,

on Friday, December 19, by

MRS. WILES.

Attractive and inexpensive Christmas presents for sale.

Numerous entertainments and sideshows.

TEA (at 1/- and 6d.) served from 4—6 p.m.

COFFEE (or TEA) and SANDWICHES (or CAKES) at 6d. served from 7—9.30 p.m.

TICKETS OF ADMISSION to the Bazaar may be obtained at the doors or previously from Miss VAUGHAN at the school.

PRICES :—THURSDAY and FRIDAY, from 3.30—6 p.m., 1/-, after 6 p.m., 6d.

SATURDAY, from 3—9 p.m., 6d.

Children under 12, half-price.

Friends of the school are earnestly requested to make the Bazaar widely known, and to urge all possible purchasers to attend.

Leaflet advertising the Christmas Bazaar for the new organ – 1913 appealing to parents and 'well-wishers of the School' for help with a three-day Bazaar 'to supply a long-felt need, viz: AN ORGAN FOR OUR SCHOOL HALL'.

Parents could help by:

1. Sending a subscription to the Organ Fund;
2. By sending goods to be sold at the Bazaar;
3. By attending the Bazaar in Person and bringing your friends;
4. By postponing the purchase of some of your Christmas presents until you have visited our Bazaar, so that you may fall an easy prey to our attractive collection.

The Bazaar successfully raised £377 for the organ, the total cost of which was £373, including the School crest and a brass plaque in memory of Thomas Chamberlen, who had died in July 1912. After several overhauls, the organ was still in use 83 years later.

Gladys Southgate (née Killick), born in November 1900, joined the School in September 1912 and recalled the life there in a letter written in 1995 when she was living in Gloucestershire. Her daughter-in-law, Jennifer Watson, was, by then, teaching in the School and her granddaughter, Louise Southgate, had been a Dolphin.

The School was divided into three – Lower School – starting with eight-year-olds in classes I, II & III. They had their own separate entrance and playground. The Middle School – classes Lower IV – A, B and C, and Lower Vth who, again, had their separate entrance and a larger play-ground for the middle and upper classes who played netball, rounders and individual games like skipping or ball games or games like 'He' or 'Touch'. The Upper School contained the Upper Vth, VI and a small Upper VIth for university entrants. These, too, had a separate entrance. Games were compulsory for each class, twice a week with gym once a week.

(All games were played on the field behind the School building until 1917, when Waring and Gillow, who owned the furniture factory at the end of Cambridge Grove, were given permission by the Governors, as a matter of patriotic duty and for a small rent, to build a large, temporary hutment cov-ering half the area, for aircraft production. These would have been some of the earliest war-planes in existence. The remaining space was devoted to growing tomatoes until the end of the war, when the field went back to games.)

Mrs Southgate remembered: 'From the Lower School on, the girls were divided into A, B or C according to ability and all learned English, French, Mathematics, History, Geography, Physics, Chemistry and Botany'.

Added to these, with a view to future careers, were Secretarial forms and a Civil Service Stream.

But all too soon the smooth running was to be interrupted. On 4 August 1914, the Great War (World War I) started. It was a time of high patriotism and strong antagonism to anything relating to Germany, and the Governors

The new organ – 1914

had no hesitation in discussing whether or not girls with German fathers should be allowed to stay in the School. This seems to have been judged, finally, on an individual basis, with at least one girl being asked to leave. Girls with German mothers seem to have been accepted without difficulty.

Because of blackout regulations and other hazards, including air raids, School hours were changed to run from 9 a.m. to 3.40 p.m. with a lunch break from 1.40–2.15.

Mrs Southgate's memories continue:

'Some girls went home to eat and returned for the afternoon session, others stayed at school where meals were served at tables in the dining hall with a teacher in charge. Other teachers had their own tables on a raised platform at the end of the dining room. Wednesday was a half-day and there was only Saturday school for girls who wanted to play games or to take part in matches with other schools – cricket, hockey, netball, tennis or rounders.

On Wednesday afternoons there were special dancing classes in winter and special swimming lessons at Bayswater public pool in summer. These, and private music lessons, cost extra although singing lessons were given free to certain classes – in the Physics laboratory!

All the girls had to be in by 9 a.m. and after this the entrances were locked and you had to ring the bell to get in.

To the left of the School buildings, adjoining Cambridge Grove, there was a botany garden where girls took turns to control one plot each term and learn the names of the plants'.

Daffodil Day – 1911

Flowers were brought to school regularly to decorate the form rooms and there was an annual competition for the best pot of home-grown daffodils.

There is no doubt that the war caused problems. With soldiers being killed by the thousands, some girls lost fathers or brothers and several were kept away by mothers who were terrified that they might be killed in the bombing raids. Other families were reduced from comfortable peacetime incomes to living on armed service pay and, with no money for fees, many girls had to be withdrawn, leaving the Governors with potentially serious financial difficulties. It was only through the skill and statesmanship of Charles Wigan, who had been a faithful and brilliant Clerk to the Governors since the School opened, that Godolphin managed to stay on an even keel and hold out until peace returned.

Despite all this, there were many cheerful moments, including the winning of the *Daily Mail* Challenge Cup for gymnastics in 1914.

Lively Dolphins win the *Daily Mail* Challenge Cup – 1914

It was now, too, that the long tradition of helping others had begun, and there was a Godolphin and Latymer ward at the Star and Garter Home for wounded servicemen which was supported solely by the girls' efforts at fund-raising. Many girls and ODs knitted balaclava helmets and scarves for the men in the trenches of France and Flanders, and there were concerts and plays to help raise funds for soldiers and sailors – and later airmen – and for refugees.

Nor did the School itself pass through the war unscathed. The *Old Dolphins' Association News* for 1918 reported: 'In the air raid of September 29th the School had an unwelcome visitant in the form of a shrapnel case which came through the roof and bounded down the middle staircase into the lower corridor, bringing with it an abundance of slates, lath and plaster. Considering that it was a three inch shell case and weighed nearly 6lbs, very much more damage might have been done and we may congratulate the School on escaping so lightly. Old Dolphins should make a point of seeing the shell case when they next visit the School'.

Ambitions were limited by the social attitudes of the time, and, despite the efforts of the Head Mistresses' Association, careers tended to be restricted to teaching, nursing and the Civil Service, although many girls went on to become secretaries at what would be personal assistant level now, and a few managed to become doctors and join other professions. Overwhelmingly, though, men and many women still considered that a woman's place was in the home, looking after a husband and bringing up a family. For those who failed to find a husband (and after the First World War there were many) there was always teaching – a field where married women were, for the most part, unacceptable.

The end of the war marked the beginning of a new era for all women. Until 1914, it was mostly in working-class families that both parents went out to work, while middle-class women stayed home, looked after their 'hubbies' and children or led a lively social life, but the movement to give them greater opportunities and, above all, the vote, was already being swept on its way by the courage of the suffragettes.

Miss Clement clearly had strong views on this and, in 1917, wrote to the Prime Minister pointing out briskly that only peers of the realm, criminals, lunatics and women were unable to vote at elections in Britain and it was time that this was put right. The skill and ability of women during that war, not only in the traditional role of nurses and carers but on the land and as munition workers or in engineering, had softened the attitude of the government towards them. It can only – and reluctantly – be assumed that it was not just pressure from the Head Mistress of Godolphin and Latymer which led to some women being granted the vote early in 1918 and that those over twenty-one obtained the full franchise in 1928.

At the eleventh hour of the eleventh day of the eleventh month of 1918 Gertrude Clement gathered everyone in the School to the hall and, to emotional cheers and tears, announced that an Armistice had been signed. The First World War had finished.

The end of that war also saw her resignation as Head Mistress. She had established the school with determination and success in peace and throughout the war, and her health had suffered from the strain. Now she needed less demanding work and joined the Ministry of Food as an Inspector for a short period before returning to full, thriving strength and becoming Head Mistress of the Queen Elizabeth School for Girls at Barnet.

Gertrude Clement retires – 1918

5

FREE DISCIPLINE

Katharine Theodora Zachary took over as Head Mistress of the School in the summer term of 1919 and shrewdly marked time until her staff and pupils had time to size her up and she had absorbed the atmosphere. By the opening of the September term she had settled in and was already beginning to establish a new order, based on what was known in the education circles of the time – with a raised eyebrow – as 'free discipline'.

'And after that address in the hall on the first morning of term, when the School was told something of what this meant, what a shock came upon us mistresses as the girls filled stairs and corridors with their voices on their way to their form rooms!' [wrote Miss Florence Pocock later.] 'However, it was an amusing as well as a disturbing experience, creating a lively awareness of the meaning of self-government.

Weekly mark-readings – with Miss Clement's stern eye and sharp tongue – were no more; grades instead of marks were allotted to show the standard of work attained; various misdemeanours had now to be checked without the aid of order marks. It was a difficult time, of course, and to some of the staff, and to some of the girls as well, an unreasonable venture.... But the School did not change its character in 1919. The best things in the tradition that had grown up during those first thirteen years were not about to be lost. The School was still asking of its Dolphins the things it had asked before – good work, a good will, the spirit of service which is freedom.

Miss Zachary came to us from twelve years of eager work in other schools to carry out here what she had learned she wanted to do, and term by term, and year by year she was pursuing her ideal.... In small matters as in large, the only achievements of value to Miss Zachary was that which came from within; an order imposed from without, such as many seek, was to her a concession, a thing to regret, though perhaps, sometimes, a stage on the way.

In planning the work for the Upper School more and more freedom of choice was made possible as years went on; what was aimed at always was that school work should mean an awakening of interests that would become a permanent influence through life.... For Miss Zachary, the

Miss Katharine Zachary – 1919

School existed as a number of personalities for whom she bore responsibility. She did not seek to give it any particular intellectual bent, but increased the number of alternative subjects for special study in the senior forms to the furthest limit of possibility.'

At a time when the more extreme educationalists were beginning to preach a different philosophy of teaching in their 'progressive' establishments, Miss Zachary already had the bit between her teeth and was experimenting with her own changes.

'Lessons for the Middle School in Literature, History, Geography, Art and

Bobbed hair and short skirt – the 'new look' Dolphin – 1923

Music were planned to show the thought and activities of men in the Renaissance period and the two earlier centuries and to create some awareness of the underlying unity of human interest that gave meaning to it all [continued Miss Pocock]. That it was a plan certainly effective in linking diligent individual work with keen enjoyment was plain enough to us who helped to carry it out, but there loomed ahead in the year following these three years, the General School Examination [followed later by O (Ordinary) Levels and then by GCEs and GCSEs] and, alas, that was ominous enough to bring the experiment to an end.'

A year after dropping her liberal bombshell, Kathleen Zachary reported to the 1920 Senior Speech Day: 'Last year, at the end of my report, I rashly undertook to try to tell you something of how far we had succeeded in our attempt to demand a higher sense of responsibility from the girls and to give them a deeper freedom'. She was not, she emphasised, demanding self-government but the government of self. 'The vast majority have, I think, been loyal and responsive to the opportunities offered to them, and are learning more fully what are the responsibilities involved by freedom and what difficulties will assail them when the guiding lines that have kept them in the straight path are taken away. Do not think for a moment that we are satisfied with the standard we have reached, but we are sufficiently encouraged to gather fresh hopes and fresh resolution for a mightier effort'; and in this, she thanked the parents for their co-operation, their encouragement for what she was trying to do and their absence of criticism.

'I feel very strongly that co-operation between the home and the School should be as close as possible ... the greater knowledge we have of the home life of the girls, the easier it is to deal wisely with them', she explained as she urged parents to let their daughters continue their education for as long as they could.

These were hard years after the stress of the war and she understood the need of an extra breadwinner which was forcing girls to start work as soon as they were legally allowed to do so. Nevertheless, she pleaded with parents, 'let your girls stay at school for as long as possible.... I feel with every fibre in my being that education cannot be hurried ... that in anything short of real necessity it is but short-sighted policy to curtail either the happy school days or the period of specialised training. Apart altogether from the undoubted fact that in the world's market the untrained goes to the wall and money spent on education and training yields compound interest in later years, education to help us must become a part of us and the response must be a deep one, not merely on the surface. We must gain the power to think for ourselves, we must avoid the disasters of shallow criticism and judgement which are, I think, the cause of so much of what is wrong in the world today. Whether we are to be teachers, artists, musicians, gymnasts or clerks or wives, the foundations must be deeply laid. It is not enough to pass examinations with brilliance or possess great speed and accuracy or understand the domestic arts, but we must have time to realise something of the possibilities of life, to get enough love for what is true and what is beautiful, to be determined to continue its pursuit all through our lives – and we cannot do this quickly'.

VIth formers in the School garden – 1920s

It was a vitally important speech inasmuch as it spelled out the whole future philosophy in which the famous 'atmosphere' of Godolphin and Latymer was founded and has grown.

As an aside, she apologised to the somewhat stunned audience of dignitaries (including the Chairman of Governors, the Bishop of Coventry, who made a speech urging the girls to take as their motto the established principles of Duty and Service which he had learned as a schoolboy at Winchester) for offering what they might have considered a too trivial report on the School's activities. Somewhat unusual it might have been, but at least – even 70 years later – it gave a flavour of the atmosphere at Iffley Road in the early twenties.

The School, she said, was quite full, with 540 pupils and many more still applying for admission. Attendance was high, the School doctor's report on the girls' health was very satisfactory and many parents had told of the benefit their daughters had gained from gymnastics, games and the regular school life.

Apart from the main examinations – London General School Certificate (at fifteen) and Matriculation (at eighteen), girls had been successful with examinations of the Royal Drawing Society, the Associated Board of the Royal Academy of Music and the Royal College of Music, and a number of girls had gained places to universities – mostly London and Oxford.

The games had aroused 'zest and enthusiasm' with the standard of play and sense of public spirit much improved. Practice for the lively and now traditional Skipping Competition between forms had provided 'a warm and happy exercise for the recreation period'. A singing competition was tried at the end of the summer term with songs chosen by a Girls' Committee whose members came from every form, with one of their number conducting. The newly formed Literary and Debating Society had met once a fortnight and

The garden front showing the Cambridge Grove gate – 1920s

'the eloquence displayed at a debate over the humiliation of wearing a stiff straw hat in windy weather has been useful in leading me to introduce the more accommodating dark blue felt hat'.

A new School Library Committee had already re-catalogued the books under a modified form of the Dewey system. Gifts for the School's fourteenth birthday had included a 'musical gong' (still hanging on the wall by the entrance to the School hall in the 1990s) presented by the staff; an old oak desk from Miss Edith Clement (sister of Gertrude); sectional bookcases for the library; a double bass for the School orchestra and a sundial engraved with the School motto. (Two of Miss Clement's sisters worked with her

The 'musical gong' – gift of the staff – 1924

during her term of office, one as an Art Mistress, the other in charge of 'housekeeping'.)

In memory of Miss Clement's period as Head Mistress (which Miss Zachary praised for the excellence of the work she had inherited and the remarkably high standard of order and obedience among the girls), the parents had decided to give an annual prize of books – and the Gertrude Clement books prize 'for girls taking an Honours course, preferably in English, at the University' is still being awarded.

Charity work was in full swing – a hundred infants from the slum Mission Parish, which G & L helped to support, had been entertained on the school field. Arriving by lorry they had, according to the newly established School Magazine, at first been totally overawed but then swarmed over the field, playing games and competitions, gorging on a huge tea and being reluctantly ushered back into their lorries and driven away, each clutching sweets and a 'big, rosy red apple' handed to them by the Head Mistress. There was constant support for the United Girls' School Mission with subscriptions and gifts of clothes; and in May every year, lilies of the valley, grown in the School grounds, were sold to raise money for St Dunstan's, a charity founded to care for ex-servicemen who had been blinded in the war.

Inspectors from the Board of Education had examined the music work and found it 'so well looked after that it was unnecessary, if not impossible, to make suggestions'. In addition to the teaching of piano, violin and singing there was a School orchestra which practised weekly; lectures on music, concerts and organ recitals. Sport included hockey, tennis and netball 'played with vigour' and the whole of the sports field would shortly be available after the aircraft factory which had covered half of it since 1917 was removed early in 1921. The Wednesday half-day afternoon was regularly used for botanical expeditions, nature study, rambles and visits to places of historical interest.

A taste of G & L in the 1920s came much later from another source. At seventy-three years old, a Mrs Frances Bibby (née Florence Hirst) decided to write down all she could remember of her childhood in West London, which included her education at G & L, starting in 1922, at the age of eight, in the Junior Department, where the younger children had their own little playground and finished ten minutes earlier than the rest of the school. She was particularly impressed by the gym teacher 'an elderly lady wearing a gym tunic down to mid-calf (it seemed funny to see a teacher wearing a gym-tunic) who told us at our first lesson that "little gels must not wear stays for gym". We had to display parts of our liberty bodices to her to check that they were not the vetoed garment'.

(Many years later, Dame Joyce Bishop recalled her battles with the family of the comedienne Hattie Jacques, who had always been amply proportioned, over the matter of not wearing stays for gym when she attended the School.)

Florence enjoyed the enormous range of books available in the 'fiction library' – a large cupboard – and the class libraries, which she thought were stocked partly from books left behind after the Boys' School had closed. Not surprisingly, her favourite authors were Henty and Ballantyne; she also enjoyed *Alice in Wonderland* and *Brer Rabbit*. Needlework meant sewing cotton bloomers or long-sleeved blouses entirely by hand, and French began with phonetics for two terms. Later, in the senior part of the School, she studied Science, with Physics in the new laboratories which were built in the late 1920s ('furnished in beautiful natural coloured wood – our life was absolute hell if any mark was made on the new benches!').

Numerous visits to the Science Museum were nerve-racking. 'Miss Bentham ... seemed convinced that she would not get us all in or out of the train before the new automatic doors closed; to deal with this problem she would split us up into teams of five or six, each with a team leader who would have to report to her after leaving or entering a train'. Nobody ever seems to have been lost.

'Out of the routine of lessons, Miss Bentham seemed quite human; on Wednesday afternoons she used to have a group of volunteers to make simple physics apparatus; I joined this group and we learnt all sorts of metal and wood-work skills while she acquired extra apparatus. Some of us also made model gliders out of balsa wood which, unfortunately, were not very successful when we tried them out on the school field. The chance to learn these skills in a girls' school of the 1920s must have been very rare indeed!'

Outings gradually extended further afield, and by 1928 three intrepid teachers, Miss Homan, Miss Mayor and Miss Phillips, set off for Paris with 20 Dolphins – aged fifteen. 'We visited so many places in that week that I have never been able to re-visit them all on any one subsequent visit', said Florence. 'Notre Dame, Sacré Coeur, the Old Luxembourg Palais exhibition of Impressionists, the Louvre, Versailles, St Cloud by boat and many other places. One evening we went to the Opera, having boxes very high up and complete with ante-rooms in each of which there was a sofa; when the opera finished we were getting ready to go back to our hotel but discovered that there was a ballet, *Salomé*, to follow. We eventually got back to our hotel, by taxi at 1 a.m'.

Although 'Doris Rackow inquired why we couldn't go to the Folies Bergère and Pearl Bridger wanted to know where the nobility had their lavatories at Versailles', most of the group accepted what they saw and enjoyed it all. More than that, for many of them, it accomplished what Miss Zachary had hoped for in starting the girls on a lifetime interest in theatre, opera, ballet and the arts which burgeoned with the inspired productions which were taking place at the old Lyric Theatre, close to the School, where the Ballet Rambert with the young Frederick Ashton, Markova and Dolin were beginning to make their reputations. From there, scores of Dolphins went on to Sadlers Wells and the Old Vic for performances by John Gielgud, Ralph Richardson, John Laurie and other contemporary 'stars', walking back home to West London when they ran out of money for their bus and tram fares.

Many of the girls, too, joined the crowds who swarmed down to the edge of the Thames, nearby, for the Oxford and Cambridge Boat Race each year. 'All the shops were full of favours which we were allowed to wear on our gym tunics; each class was divided into the two lots of supporters and we played hockey and netball games with Oxford v Cambridge teams'.

Florence's family was always short of money but she managed to stay on into the VIIth form to take the entrance exam for Cambridge – with Oxford as a reluctant second choice. (She gained a scholarship to Girton.) There were only about a dozen girls, and Miss Zachary, who acted as their form mistress, would drop in for a chat. 'We always thought she was a rather lonely woman who would have liked to have had the same easy relationship with her pupils that many of her staff did, but we found it difficult to recover from the image of a rather forbidding woman that we had acquired lower down the School'.

It was during these chats that the Head explained her 'unorthodox' ways of running the School. She had been educated as a boarder at the Godolphin School in Salisbury which, at that time, had very strict rules on everything, including school uniform so, at eighteen, she had no idea how to choose clothing for herself. 'She would say "I left school at eighteen with no idea on even how to choose a hat" and as she still chose large brimmed hats that appeared to be mobile fruit and flower shops, we felt that she hadn't learned since'.

It was in these chats, too, that they discussed the state of the world at that time, when the whole of Europe was recovering from the war and the impact of the Russian Revolution, and many countries, including Britain, were in dire economic straits. In 1926 conditions were so bad that a General Strike had been called and was tersely referred to in the Magazine of that year:

Walking
Talking
Wireless
Fireless.

Wireless had already been in the School for three years, thanks to a gift from a Dr Soar which provided enough money to cover the initial expenses. 'We promptly applied for a licence', reported the School Magazine for 1923. 'After a long time the Postmaster General informed us that he considered that we were fit and proper persons to receive one'. The School bought a crystal set and 'a few miles of wire which we proceeded to wind on cardboard cylinders. We already have our aerial up and we hope to be ready to receive music, weather reports, parliamentary speeches and other interesting items at half term. Everybody is most enthusiastic and only too willing to be initiated into the mysteries of wave-lengths, valves and such technical terms'.

The twenties were a difficult time, with many families, determined that they had finished a war which must end all wars, stubbornly turning their faces away from the possibility of any further conflict and into a form of

Science laboratories adjoined the new Godolphin Library – 1927

escapism, for their children at least. The magazine for those postwar years was filled with poems and stories about fairies, elfin adventures and knights with fair ladies. Many of the illustrations had an ethereal feeling and had titles like *The key to God's Fairyland* and *It was night and the stars were peeping where God had hung them afar*. . . .

Already, the immense individual caring side of the School was being built up. Florence recalls one girl who was regularly attacked by her mother, coming to school embarrassed by a black eye or scratched and torn face. Eventually, in desperation, she ran away from home – and School – only to be taken to court for stealing. Miss Zachary made a special journey to Brighton for the hearing, spoke up for her so that she was bound over, and brought her back to live with a friend of the Botany teacher, helping with the housework and children and learning shorthand and typing so that eventually she was able to get work.

A new Art teacher was appointed at this time 'a real artist who had London Transport posters, done by her, on the trains; she looked very "arty" as she came to School in a black cloak and a large hat'. Many of the girls she taught went on to art college.

There was no doubting the self-governing element of School. 'We voted for form captains, the VIth form voted for the School Captain, we had numerous clubs, each of which had its committees formed from form representatives who were voted for and who, in turn, elected officers who all had their jobs to do. The general discipline was relaxed for those days, speaking allowed in the corridors and cloakrooms, no going from class to class in lines.

Seniors could use unsupervised cloakrooms, could come into School early and stay late, working in the library until 6 p.m.

'If, however, you broke this trust or behaved in a way unbecoming for a senior, then you lost these privileges, had to use cloak-rooms with the juniors, do prep at the back of a class and feel very degraded'.

By now a School uniform, a navy blue tunic, had been instituted, but the Upper VIth were not expected to wear this and there was no mention of it in the Prospectus. They were, however, responsible for helping out with the younger forms.

The new Godolphin Library was opened in 1927

The School was still full and flourishing, so that in 1926 they could announce the opening of the new Godolphin Library, built to a design which copied a wing of the old Godolphin House in Cornwall, with mullioned windows above and an open cloister below which was later enclosed with glass sliding doors and used as a classroom.

At the same time, gifts of books began to pour in – many of them from Dolphins as leaving presents.

By 1930, the postwar euphoria was beginning to wear thin and by 1931 the girls and staff were joining together to form a branch of the junior League of Nations organisation, aimed as a positive step towards preserving peace. At the same time, Hitler was forming his National Socialist party – the Nazis – in Germany, and in London politicians were convincing the electorate that there would be no future war.

For anyone who suggests that these were the halcyon years of endless long

59

White tiles lined the lower corridor until the wood panelling of the 1960s

The new botany garden – 1920s

hot summers, the Magazine for 1931–32 included *A Schoolgirl's Song*:

Where is the sun that we all used to love,
As it shone down on earth from its home up above?
Is there no sunshine behind all the rain?
Oh, will we never see summer again?
We longed for a day we could really call 'warm'
Just to bring out our racquets and hie to the lawn,
Yet all it did was to rain just the same,
Even rounders were doomed. How we longed for a game!

School outing – 1930s

More girls were gaining places, exhibitions and scholarships to Universities – Oxford, Cambridge and London – as the life of the School expanded. The choirs took part in music festivals with other London schools; parties of girls attended the Robert Mayer Concerts for children in the Central Hall, Westminster; the fine tradition of School plays which had started in the earliest days continued with major productions; the Literary Society discussed Kipling and Dickens; the Science Society visited the Cherry Blossom boot polish factory, the waterworks at Barnes, the Women's Printing Society.

Ominously, the Debating Society discussed the advisability of applying military sanctions to Italy, and the League of Nations Union listened to a talk on 'Refugees and the Save the Children Fund'. The Nazi persecution of the Jews started and a wave of Jewish families began to leave Germany. In the same year, 1935, the School 'adopted' a fourteen-year-old Russian boy, Alexander Baranovsky, who was living in Poland. Some girls went to meetings at the Albert Hall on the Italian–Abyssinian War and lectures on the present-day situation in Europe.

In 1935, the School faced its own crisis, reported on the opening page of the 1935 Magazine:

> Miss Zachary is leaving! We have all repeated the words but we cannot realise the truth. For, to us, Miss Zachary and the Godolphin traditions are inseparable and it seems that if she leaves, the School will depart with her.... For many years she has worked devotedly for the School, helping and strengthening us both as individuals and as a community. Our gratitude to her can never be adequately expressed, yet we all know that although the School may have many Headmistresses, there can never be another Miss Zachary...

True though this was, a new and potentially even greater Head Mistress, Miss (later Dame) Joyce Bishop was waiting in the wings to embark on another memorable period in the history of the School.

6

MISS BISHOP TAKES OVER

Nobody who knew Dame Joyce Bishop as a sprightly ninety-year-old, erect, bubbling with life and energy, beautifully groomed grey hair curling softly round a vibrantly expressive face lit by piercing blue eyes, could have recognised the description of her quoted in the *Portrait of a Headmistress* by one of her former pupils, Sheila Rose. '...I was a very delicate child, suffering four severe bouts of pneumonia and one horrific attack of meningitis during which I was unconscious for six weeks and not expected to survive'.

They would certainly have understood the next sentence: 'I must have had an intense desire to live...'

From the moment of her birth in Birmingham on 28 July 1896 until her death in 1993, Joyce Bishop devoted her powerful talent not only to living life to its fullest intensity, but in persuading others to do the same.

'Perhaps it is because I have a foot in two centuries that the past and the traditions of any place or community with which I have been closely associated have been so important to me, and while I have welcomed the exciting opportunities of exploring and playing a very small part in the astounding changes which have taken place, and have fought for and applauded most of the increased opportunities for women in our society and enjoyed and marvelled at the amazing development in the facilities of travel and the resulting opportunities of improved communications with peoples everywhere, my acceptance and involvement in the change – especially in the world of education – has been determined by my conviction that the change has been evolved from something of fundamental value in the past and not by destruction of that value.'

Joyce Bishop was the middle and much loved child of a comfortably-off Midlands manufacturer who not only conducted a flourishing business but had wide and deep cultural and intellectual interests. For a brief spell as a small girl she was sent to a local kindergarten, but she was away so often through ill health that her mother decided a governess would be better for her. Accordingly, the governess was installed to give lessons, which Joyce later described as 'dull and consisted of learning tables by heart – I was good at that – and a lot of spelling and history... and some very inspired religious

Dame Joyce Bishop at eighty years with one of her favourite small dogs (Courtesy The Froebel Institute)

teaching which I found most satisfying after all the terror and excitement of the Old Testament stories and *Pilgrim's Progress*'.

At nine, her health strengthened enough for her to be able to go to Edgbaston High School, where she spent 'ten radiantly happy years' and where, on one morning, she took along her angora rabbit for an outing, hoping to keep it on or in her desk during lessons. It was here, too, despite her head mistress's less than enthusiastic welcome for rabbits in school, that she determined to become a head mistress herself.

Once again, her health was to stand in her way. In her third year she began to go deaf and 'for two years I suffered real agony from wrong treatment... the most distinguished ear specialist in Birmingham failed to discover the cause of the trouble until, at last, after two years of misery and almost complete deafness the truth revealed itself in the shape of a polypus'.

This dealt with, she was cured and revelled once more in school life (apart from Mathematics, which she failed in the Higher Certificate Examination and had to retake). 'It is queer to think of the sophisticated young today and to remember one's own passionate desire not to grow up, not to leave school and, although I was going up to Oxford in October 1915, I wept to think that it was the end of my golden age'.

Lady Margaret Hall at the height of the First World War was not offering the traditional ebullient undergraduate life. Most of the men were either training for war or leaving to join battalions. But the young Joyce Bishop found plenty to absorb her time – almost too much, as apart from studying, she and her fellow undergraduates found themselves digging potato fields in the Parks, tying up stretchers for the wounded at the Front or serving in canteens for munition workers, 'and always, outside the door of the dining hall ... the appallingly long casualty lists, posted daily, so often bringing news of some irreparable loss to almost each of us'.

Unhappily, the double stress of work and war took its toll. 'On the third day of my final Schools examination, I missed my special paper, wrote one in my own room and fainted at the Sheldonian after a brief attempt at another'. She refused to apply for an aegrotat or to stay on for a further year to retake her finals. 'It seemed urgent to begin teaching with so many posts vacant owing to the casualties in France'. Instead, she accepted 'a deplorable third' with an accompanying letter from her examiners explaining what they would have expected her to achieve, based on her normal standard of work. Her prospective employers were more concerned with the woman than the degree and she began her career teaching English at the Hertfordshire and Essex High School. 'I was very happy there and I don't quite know why, at the age of twenty-seven, I persuaded myself with extraordinary presumption that I was ready to apply for a headship', she wrote later.

Before going to Oxford, she had helped her aunt to organise events at a club for factory girls in Birmingham, so she had some experience of the hardships of working-class life in an industrial city. Now, her older sister Phyllis, who had been the first head mistress of the new and enterprising Holly Lodge High School for Girls at Smethwick, was retiring to get married. There was only one person she could trust to continue her pioneering work and so it was that, at twenty-seven, Miss Bishop returned to the Midlands as a head mistress.

Smethwick, on the edge of the Black Country around Birmingham, was a highly industrialised town with many advantages and even more dis-

advantages, with its prosperous foundries, glass works, breweries and malt-
ings on one hand and on the other, mean streets, poor housing, grinding
poverty and an overall smell which was powerful and penetrating.

The school was two years old and the pupils were admitted entirely on
merit from the poorest homes in the town when the new young Head
arrived. 'Most of the fathers were out of work; their clothes were pawned,
they had nothing to stand up in and they could not go to the Labour
Exchange to seek a job. For the girls at Holly Lodge, school was the best
thing they had met. Their education was tremendously prized'. The Chairman of Governors was a small-town draper who had been born in a work-
house and had educated himself by reading widely and deeply. He had
persuaded the local council to buy 22 acres of land with an old Victorian
mansion in the middle of it. This was the new school.

It was here, surrounded by dreary streets, fish and chip shops, a railway
and a brewery, that the girls 'with good brains and tremendous zest and
determination' set to work. Joyce Bishop worked with them, leading them
not only through the curriculum but through plays, music and poetry into a
world which many of them thought of as Paradise. Despite the economic
problems of the 1920s and the delays caused by the General Strike, she
managed to have a new school building, complete with Science labs, Art
room, pottery and gymnasium built and ready for occupation by September
1926. All this in opposition to the activities of the local Education Officer,
who, she declared, knew nothing about education. 'I was a very young Head
Mistress and he thought that if he bound me tightly in red tape I should be
less likely to give trouble. He did not know that I was allergic to red tape
and simply had to find ways of cutting through it. The poor man died after I
had been there for 18 months, not, I am glad to say, because of my resistance
to the red tape but from natural causes.

'When I left in 1935, we had nine girls at Oxford and Cambridge and
many more at provincial universities and Teacher Training Colleges', she
wrote. 'Very many went on to do something other than clerical work –
nursing, teaching, pharmacy, physiotherapy and so on'. (At Dame Joyce's
memorial service in St Margaret's Church, Westminster, an elderly white-
haired lady slipped in quietly to join the packed congregation. She had, she
said, been one of 'Miss Bishop's' earliest pupils and was paying a last tribute
to the inspired woman to whom she owed her Oxford degree and a life's
career as a Classics teacher.)

The full story of Dame Joyce Bishop's life is recounted by Sheila Rose, but
it was clear, even as she walked into Godolphin and Latymer for the September term of 1935, elegantly dressed and, to the shocked surprise of some
of her older colleagues, sporting a discreet but distinct and daring trace of
powder and lipstick, that this was no ordinary Head Mistress. Like so many
others, she faced the hard task of replacing a much loved, long-established
and respected previous Head, but there was no doubt, from the word 'go',

that she would waste no time in doing this.

'I stepped like Agag in most matters during my first and second years', she admitted later. 'There were eight members of staff who had given 25 or more years of service to the School and the most splendid people they were. I felt they must accept me and love me before I ventured on any new plans'.

In many ways, life in my new school was very different: it had been richly blessed in having two distinguished Headmistresses before me, people who had built up sound traditions of scholarship and established a very individual pattern of non-competitive, co-operative activity based on an ideal of self-discipline. There existed a minimum of rules and a maximum, of responsibility. It was a fee-paying school with about 40 per cent of scholarship places filled by girls who had gained the old LCC [London County Council] Junior County Scholarships, and there were a few LCC Supplementary Scholars who came in at thirteen and some girls from Middlesex who had been awarded free places. The girls represented a good cross-section of society, though very few touched the level of poverty I had met in Smethwick'.

'There was no Preparatory Department', she recalled in the 1980s. (Until then there had been younger girls, but as part of the main school.) 'I persuaded the Governors to increase the number of local free places to twelve and to open a Preparatory Department in what had been the Head Mistress's house and in which I did not wish to live. The Preparatory was for children from four to ten and very soon we had a happy little community, nearly all the members of which later came up into the main school. Many of them today are amongst the most distinguished Old Dolphins representing all walks of life from film stars to top-ranking mathematicians and classicists. I believed passionately in the importance of the Preparatory Department: it was good for the older girls to have these very young children about and it was very good for the ones who came up to have, from the beginning, the right attitude to discipline and learning'.

Not only had Godolphin and Latymer profited from the regimes of two good head Mistresses, but, following the somewhat dilatory Trustees (and later, Governors) of the Godolphin Boys' School, had benefited enormously from a series of dedicated Governors, – women as well as men – almost all of whom could be relied on to attend Governors' meetings and give whole-hearted attention to the needs of the School. No longer, now, were there notes in the Minutes 'meeting abandoned – insufficient in attendance to form a quorum'.

'They were educated men and women with a real understanding of the right values in education', explained the new Head. 'They gave me freedom to run the School in the way I thought best but were always at hand if needed. There was no interference from any educational official and the Clerk [Charles Wigan], whose father had served the School before him, looked after the building and gave legal advice when asked and at all times gave an unfailing friendliness and courteous consideration to all my problems.

67

Jubilee juniors in the new 'princess line' gymslips – 1935

I was especially grateful for his refreshing freedom from all taint of bureaucracy and his conspicuous neglect of the use of red tape'.

As for Godolphin and Latymer – in its first Magazine following her appointment, the Editorial reported: 'This year we have welcomed to the School Miss Bishop who, in a short time, has made herself a friend of both present and old Dolphins. . . . We should like here to extend official welcome to a new Dolphin in the person of Woggs, who, whether gambolling on the field or reposing in the office, seems thoroughly to enjoy his membership of the School'. Woggs was to be the first of a succession of small dogs – usually cairn terriers or Jack Russells – who accompanied Miss Bishop throughout her period at Godolphin and, indeed, until the end of her long life.

It was not the most comfortable time for living or planning ahead. Again the Debating Society was discussing the advisability of applying military sanctions to Italy – which, under the Fascist leadership of Benito Mussolini, was attacking Abyssinia not only with traditional weapons but with poison gas. ('Girls seemed reluctant to state their views and were not sufficiently acquainted with the subject to be able to speak with confidence', reported the School Magazine'. 'At the next meeting they were well within their depth, for the subject of the debate was that age-old topic "should homework be abolished?" ').

There had been two particularly popular showings of sound films which had replaced the earlier silent cinematograph. *Northern Lights* and *Young Things* had attracted more than 300 girls, including some Upper IIIs, instead of the normal attendance of around 60.

Social Service notes reported that collections had been made in School for the Alexandra Rose Day and for Invalid Children's Aid, as well as preparations for the Christmas Party, held every year for children from the slums. Sweets, toys and fruit were brought to School and 250 stockings were stuffed with 'delightful surprises'. There was enthusiastic support for the funds which provided holidays in the country for children from the Foundling Site and for many needy girls in London. It was in 1935, too, that a party from School went to the Annual Service of the United Girls' Schools Association in St Martin-in-the-Fields church. The preacher, who spoke fervently of the problems of inequality of opportunity, was a distinguished churchman, Dr A Herbert Gray, pacifist and founder of the Marriage Guidance Council. Some 30 years later his daughter, Margaret, was to follow Joyce Bishop as the fourth Head Mistress of Godolphin and Latymer.

It was a period of uncertainty and upheaval, nationally and internationally. King George V died and the Chairman of the School Governors, Sir Marshall Hays, arranged for a party of Dolphins to watch the State funeral procession from the balcony of the Cocoa Tree Club in Piccadilly. Already there were shocked rumours that the new King, Edward VIII, was involved with an American divorcee. The School echoed with such scurrilous chants as 'Hark the herald angels sing – Mrs Simpson's got our King'. The rumours

Biology space was shared with music in the mid-1930s

proved all too true and were followed swiftly by Edward's abdication and the accession and coronation of his younger brother, George VI. The headlines billowed with stories of the scandal of the young King who was never crowned, and then of the family of the new monarch and his young daughters – the Princesses Elizabeth and Margaret Rose.

But in the background once more, was the shadow of war. Mussolini, still campaigning in Abyssinia, was joining in unholy alliance with Adolf Hitler, the Fuehrer of the German National Socialist Party – the Nazis – already embarked on his campaign to provide *Lebensraum* for the Germans by marching into their neighbouring countries. In Spain there was a bloody civil war, at the peak of which the small city of Guernica was mercilessly bombed from the air. The slaughter of its civilian population was memorably recorded by the artist Pablo Picasso, and the British government was forced, at last, to admit that the Great War of 1914–18 might not, after all, have ended all wars.

By 1938, plans for the civil defence of Britain's cities were already in hand. High on the list of priorities was the evacuation of all the schoolchildren in London whose parents wished them to be taken off to safety in the country. Schools were sent introductions on What To Do in what was euphemistically dubbed 'An Emergency'. Briefly, as the Prime Minister, Neville Chamberlain, went to Munich to negotiate with Herr Hitler, London's schoolchildren braced themselves to leave their homes and families, but Chamberlain flew home to report 'peace in our time', and the September term started on time, if uneasily.

A year later Hitler was poised to march into Poland. A final ultimatum went out from Britain urging him to hold back and reconsider, but to no effect. On 1 September 1939, as German tanks set off for the Polish border, nearly half London's schoolchildren – 241,000 boys and girls – were evacuated from the capital. On Sunday 3 September, Britain declared war on Germany. Within minutes, the first air raid sirens wailed into life with an ominous fanfare for the Second World War which was to last for nearly six years.

7

DOLPHINS AT WAR

As the politicians argued and negotiated, London's children had abandoned their summer holiday and spent the last two weeks of August waiting in their schools, playing, talking, racing round and wondering whether, yet again, this would be a false alarm. Miss Bishop had called Godolphin and Latymer parents to the hall to explain what might happen and to ask for volunteer mothers to help if the evacuation went ahead.

Years later, one of the mothers chosen to help, Mrs E M Cox, left the school a report with the hope 'that my description of the Dolphins in the war days may be of some interest...'

This time there were no false alarms. The first of September was warm and sunny, as London was transformed at the start of a glowing Indian summer. From every street, children set off for school and then the railway stations. As train after train slid in, empty and desolate, they climbed aboard with no idea of where they were going or whether they would see their families again. Dolphins were among them.

'After a short talk by Miss Bishop we fell into line and started out for Ravenscourt Park station with mixed feelings, as one can imagine [wrote Mrs Cox]. My husband, who had urged me to volunteer, and my father, mingled with the crowd waiting to see the School depart but, they did not allow us to see them for fear that we should all break down ... feelings were very near the surface that day as the children of London went through the streets into the unknown.

We had imagined that we were bound for the West Country but, to our surprise, the train stopped at Windsor and we were told to get out. Like a cloud of locusts a party of very energetic voluntary workers descended upon us, gave each of us a carrier bag with corned beef, tinned milk etc and carried us off in a most haphazard fashion. Eventually our party found themselves in the playground of Sunningdale School – some girls had actually been whisked off to Eton College!

All was confusion but, at last, I was given a list of householders who had promised to take in schoolchildren and, accompanied by about a dozen girls of varying ages, began our pathetic trek down a long country lane where there were large, detached houses with long drives up to the front porches.

1 September 1939 – leaving Iffley Road

Alas, when we had trailed up the drives we had very sorry receptions. Most of the charming ladies who opened the doors apologised for being unable to take a girl as they had promised because their sister, or cousin, or niece was coming to stay. One or two did keep their word and we said goodbye to the lucky girls who had found shelter. It began to grow dark and drizzle and soon I found myself burdened with several carrier bags from which the handles had parted and the contents had fallen into the road. The spirits of the party fell and even I began to feel dejected.

Finally we struck lucky – a retired Naval Commander and his daughter decided that they would take seven girls – but we had eight! The energetic daughter looked them over and decided to take them all because my youngest daughter was small. I handed over the carrier bags and promised to return in the morning to make proper arrangements. My daughters called out 'but where are you going to sleep?' I couldn't think what to answer and they were hustled indoors and finally went to bed in the servants' attic, weeping because they thought I would be sleeping in a hedge.

A passing motorist stopped and asked me where I was going and I had to say I didn't know. Eventually he said I could put up for the night in his house, but for no longer as his mother-in-law would not have refugees! I slept on a camp bed in the lounge and in the morning was awakened by a Nannie bringing in a small girl who wanted to see what a refugee looked like. My host told me I could not stay in the house but I could camp in the coppice in a tent, so for the next three nights I slept in the little wood with a toad and rabbits for company.'

73

In the morning, after establishing that the girls were to gather in the playground of Sunningdale School to discover what was to happen next, she returned to the home of the Naval Commander. Here, all the girls were being treated as servants and given housework to do. Her daughters were cleaning the silver. 'They were treated quite kindly by their hosts, but certainly not as equals. They were not allowed to play on the lawn or use the front entrance, nor were they encouraged to play with the two children of the family, Master James and Miss Belinda'. Master James, however, had other ideas and soon had the girls climbing rickety rope ladders into the trees while using 'mild swear words' to encourage them.

Meanwhile, Miss Bishop had hired a taxi and was hurtling round the area trying to discover what had happened to her girls. 'It was dreadful', she said, recalling it many years after the war. 'I was responsible for all the girls and yet I had no idea where they had been found homes, nor with whom.

In the Jubilee Book of the School, published in 1955, she described evacuation from her side of the picture:

On 1 September 1939, some 400 children and all the staff left this building and set forth on the unknown adventure of evacuation. We had imagined many things; we had planned – so we thought – for every eventuality and had steeled our minds and bodies to meet undismayed whatever the engines of destruction might rain upon us. And then it was all rather an anti-climax. Our journey was very short – merely as far as Windsor, whither we travelled in complete safety and comfort.

There, our troubles began, but while we thought we could face bravely dire peril and calamity, it was difficult merely to control the temper when stupid and overbearing officials broke up our carefully organised plans and thrust girls indiscriminately into buses going I knew not whither. It is true that they were taken no further than the wilds of Bucks and Berks, but that first night of the blackout no one could tell me where they were, nor would anyone penetrate the blackness to find them, so that I suffered agonies of mind as I imagined them unloved and unwanted in outlandish places.

These imaginings were fostered by what had actually happened to my own contingent, which had been dropped in Ascot where no billeting lists had been revised since the previous September and where householders had been led to expect a party of expectant mothers – not schoolgirls varying in age from nine to nineteen. Doors were opened to our knocking, only to be shut in horror when what was standing on the step was seen. Darkness had long since fallen when the last child was finally housed.

Then followed three weeks of almost unbroken sunshine, of picnics and excursions for the girls and of difficulties indescribable and innumerable for the staff.

The School was in five different places, but in not one of them was there a school building we could use, so that it was obvious that a further move would have to be made — obvious to me but not to officialdom who, at that stage, felt that having got us out of London not much more could be expected of it. Girls came and girls went, billets were found and lost, some householders in large mansions enquired suspiciously what manner of thing this secondary schoolgirl might be, and looked distastefully upon it when it was produced or described. Much had to be explained, much contrived, but for the little unkindness, much kindness was found and by the time the various Ministries had been persuaded that we must be moved to Newbury where a school would give us accommodation, at any rate for part of every day, many girls had formed firm friendships with their kind hostesses and left them with much reluctance.

Evacuation — arriving at Newbury complete with small brothers — 1939 (Courtesy Hammersmith and Fulham Archive and Local History Collection)

It was, indeed, a nightmare for the Head and for her staff, not least Vera Titmuss, upon whose shoulders much of the organisation had fallen. Not only had billets to be found once more for all 400 girls but the school which could offer them accommodation would have to share the classrooms. For Dolphins, the school day would begin at 1 p.m. The problem of occupying the girls throughout the morning varied from visits to Woolworths to hostesses who encouraged them to stay in bed until noon to keep them out of the way. Eventually, the teachers managed to find corners where they could teach small groups of older girls who were coming up for their State examinations.

'The beauties of the classics and of English literature, the mysteries of science and mathematics and the finer shades of style in French and German were dwelt upon in unlikely places, but the winning of nine university scholarships and three State scholarships during the four years of evacuation shows, I think, that our standards were unimpaired', Miss Bishop wrote later. 'Before the end of the first year, we had secured, for the morning, the use of two large rooms over a bank. We were also allowed to sing in a large room adjoining the vicarage and to study the Scriptures in the Parish Church. We soon got a hostel established but the Ministry of Health seemed unaware that anything was needed in a hostel apart from beds and bedding. The school caretaker and his wife, Mr & Mrs Atkins, eventually came down to help run the hostel and very soon an extremely happy little community was established there'. In 1940, however, Mr & Mrs Atkins, had to return to London as the school in Iffley Road faced the onslaught of the blitz.

Later, a second hostel was opened and the school library transported to Newbury, where it was housed in a gallery of the Newbury Public Library.

Advanced science classes continued in the Physics and Chemistry laboratories which had been loaned by the local Boys' Grammar School and, although time and facilities were very limited, the Science staff managed not only to teach but to organise an exhibition in the local town hall to raise money for War Savings.

With the girls living in billets or hostels, it was not easy to organise the clubs and activities which they had enjoyed in Iffley Road, but, said Miss Bishop 'the girls enjoyed doing many things they had never done before, such as delivering newspapers, helping to collect salvage, making camouflage netting, picking strawberries and raspberries, planting leeks in a market garden and working on the school allotment which supplied both hostels with vegetables'.

On the face of it, the School was now well-organised, and near-normal work was being carried on efficiently, but being away from home put an enormous strain both on the Dolphins and their teachers – not to mention their Head. 'The girls missed their homes and their parents grievously', she wrote. 'Even kind foster parents could not entirely take the place of the girls' own parents, and where there was a lack of imagination and understanding, there was often a feeling of loneliness and unwantedness and the younger ones missed the daily encouragement which comes from a parent's interest in work and progress.

'Then, during the bad raids, many were tormented by anxiety for their parents and the older ones felt they should be sharing the danger. We knew how much the parents were missing the joy of watching their children's development and we knew that, in some cases, children were growing away from their parents and there would need to be careful adjustments on their return.

'But for the majority, evacuation deepened their love and appreciation of home and of their own school building, while developing a robust independence and initiative. Many who had not known the country learnt to love it. Who will ever forget the magical transformation of the landscape by the ice-storm and the great frost of 1940 when we woke to find a crystal world out of a Hans Andersen fairy tale, or the great drifts of giant snowdrops and wild daffodils in the spring, or the radiant days after Dunkirk and the enchanted colour and unreal quiet of the country? And we learnt a more sympathetic understanding of other people's way of life.

'In the school I think we gained a deeper knowledge of each other which will be of lasting value to us. We learned to improvise, we developed a clearer sense of what is fundamental and important and we learnt that it is not by the machinery of timetables and curricula and pre-arranged plans that what is most important in the school may be kept alive, for these are only temporary necessities which time may break or alter. But in a school, as in a nation or individual, that which links the chaotic present to the past, that which give us hope, whatever may be in store in the future, is the inner life which is not the butt of circumstance and outward change, but which survives all these by virtue of its dependence upon God'.

While the main force of Dolphins was enduring life in the safety of the country, what became known as the 'Little School' was developing back at Iffley Road. The dread of immediate bombing which had shuddered through the country as the sirens moaned their air raid warning on that first Sunday of the war, had faded. Slowly, throughout the period of what became known as 'the phoney war' before the blitz with its intensive bombing of London began in September 1940, some parents decided that they might as well bring their daughters back home – even if there was no school available for them.

In May 1940, led by Miss Bryan and later Miss Pocock, classes opened for the Preparatory School and the first two years of the main School course and then, gradually, as year succeeded year, more age groups were added. To modern ears it must sound like mayhem, but many of the girls who attended the Little School remembered it as the happiest of times.

'Despite the raids and days spent in the School's air raid shelters and the necessary cutting of curricula and activities, they enjoyed the intimacy of the School's family life and they had the inspiring leadership of Miss Pocock and Miss Bryan and all the kind friendliness and courage of those two or three other staff who helped them', wrote Miss Bishop.

They were never daunted. On 15 October 1940 at the Governors' Meeting, Charles Wigan, the Clerk, reported: 'On 16 September three incendiary bombs were dropped on the School premises, one bomb fell on the inner playground and one in the top corridor on the granolithic floor – neither of these did much damage. The third fell in a classroom and some of the flooring had to be hacked out. When this happened, Waring and Gillows Depository, which adjoins the School grounds [at the top of Cambridge Grove] was gutted and 32 fire engines which crossed the School field to deal with that fire did considerable damage to the property in the field, breaking down all the tennis standards.

'On 9 October a time bomb was dropped in the corner of the inner playground near the gymnasium. [Legend has it that this happened in the blackout as the schoolkeeper, Mr Atkins, was touring the building, opening the windows against possible blast after the air raid siren had sounded. He discovered what, in the darkness, he mistook for a vaulting horse, carelessly left upended in the courtyard close to the gym. Easing round it, he opened more windows before squeezing back and continuing his rounds. Minutes later, the 'horse' exploded.] The blast blew the changing room through the gymnasium leaving nothing but a large gap in the gym wall, but with the two ends of the gymnasium still standing and most of the apparatus unharmed. The walls of the new Domestic Science room were cracked, all the windows on the north side of the School were blown out and a piece of radiator was hurled through the ceiling of one of the upper form rooms. The bomb was so powerful that its explosion left a 20 foot crater in the courtyard'.

In the face of all this, Mr Wigan was able calmly to end his report: 'At present the tutorial classes are continuing as the south side of the building is undamaged, but unless the heating apparatus can shortly be repaired it will soon be too cold to continue work in the building'.

In February 1941 a Rest Centre (to house anyone made homeless from bombing in the surrounding area) invaded the lower corridor and commandeered all the rooms on the ground floor, pushing the children upstairs to the presumably less safe first floor.

The Head continued the saga: 'The staff were undaunted and set about making the first floor into a complete school building, turning the double classroom [now the Computer room] into an attractive assembly hall and even transforming the room above the Head Mistress's office, which was now occupied by strange officials, into a friendly little room where I could see parents when I came up each week.

'The Rest Centre consisted of a great many officials who turned this ecclesiastical looking hall into something resembling a riverside café, classrooms into kitchens, dormitories and gasproof rooms, first aid rooms, etc. But there were never any inmates, never anyone who came to rest. The kitchen and dining hall were taken over by the Londoners' Meals Service, which provided innumerable meals for the public for a period of over two years'.

With the Little School being forced into smaller and smaller space, the Chairman of Governors rode to the rescue when the powers that be decided to requisition the playing-field for allotments. The gym was already a heap of rubble (thanks more to an inept Heavy Rescue Squad than the German bombers – they managed to strip off the entire roof and cast all the equipment into a heap, which caused immense postwar difficulties of claiming compensation to rebuild the gym in the name of War Damage). There was nowhere else for games or PT so the allotments remained undug and the field stayed intact.

The intensity of the blitz gradually subsided and by July 1942 many more parents and girls were tired of evacuation. The numbers in Newbury, which had been the largest of any London girls' school, began to fall. To save further disintegration it was decided that the bulk of the School should be reunited in Iffley Road, leaving a very small section running in Newbury under the leadership first of Miss Hill and later Mrs Bell.

It was the School's turn to squeeze now. With 400 pupils needing space, the apparently unwanted Rest Centre was moved out in February 1943, keeping only one cupboard as a store for blankets, bedding and emergency rations.

At about this time, Newbury suffered its first (and, as it transpired, its only) serious air raid, and the last Dolphins said farewell to their hostesses and to Miss Berwick, the Newbury County School head mistress, her staff and pupils before returning to a united G & L, now 530 strong, in Hammersmith.

It is hard to understand how adaptable and uncomplaining the staff and Dolphins had to be during the whole of this period of evacuation, but some idea of its enormity comes through clearly in Joyce Bishop's last report to the Governors from Newbury:

The summer term was a happy one. During the good weather in June and the beginning of July, the girls grew visibly browner every day. They spent every available free minute swimming in the baths or canal. They picked strawberries, weeded onions, planted leeks and helped to make camouflage netting for important Government buildings. They dug, planted, weeded and hoed an allotment of 50 poles and the results of their labours were magnificent – 20 cwt of potatoes, large quantities of carrots, turnips, beetroots, cabbages, marrows, beans – enough to feed the two hostels until the spring, I hope. The Guides camped in a lovely old barn at East Garston and did useful work, including telephone duty at the local hospital.

During the last month of term we saved £465 which we hope bought an ambulance, 2 parachutes, 2 rubber dinghies and 10 stretchers. Total amount of War Savings over £2,000.

The girls got up various concerts and plays – one extremely good concert was given at the end of the term by the VIIth and Upper VIth, who were leaving, and in addition to all this, they worked at their lessons to some effect as I hope the examination results show.

A Sick Bay was opened which serves all the schools evacuated to Berkshire and has already been of great service to us.

Staff had staggered holidays of three weeks each during the five week summer holiday when many of the children went home. Autumn Term began on 9 September but for weeks before there was the feverish nightmare of searching for new billets, not only for new children but for those whose old hostesses had tired of them. In all, 94 billets were found, largely due to the untiring efforts of Miss Titmuss, whose work in this direction is deserving of the highest praise.

During the holidays all the Newbury School cleaners were called up, so the girls of the two schools now undertake the cleaning between them – we sweep and Newbury dusts.

The third year VIth is bigger than it has been since I came – 12 girls reading for University scholarships. The numbers in the Upper Vth have gone down. There is still a large Preparatory Department of over 40, including five little boys!

Activities this term include blackberrying and jam-making. I am now registered as a Jam Manufacturer.

(This last addition to the multi-talented Miss Bishop's qualifications would have been sought so that she might qualify for an extra ration of sugar for jam-making, presumably for the girls in the hostels.)

Inevitably, there were reminiscences. Mrs Cox recalled the School being offered a large house by a wealthy woman who described it as her 'little summer-house'. It was accepted with gratitude – only to discover that it had a strong local reputation for being haunted. As the Dolphins – ranging in age from a VIth former studying for medicine to the youngest who was still in the Prep department – waited in hope and fear of seeing the ghosts, 'my host asked if he could take me to the house as he wanted to see if he could sense anything uncanny. We wandered round the pleasant rooms and they did not appear to be spook-ridden, but he said that it would be wise if we exorcised the spirits, which we solemnly did!' The house was only sparsely furnished and the Godolphin mothers scoured out some coal buckets and made cardboard lids for them in which to steam puddings as there were no large saucepans. The only crockery appeared to be 18 very large flowered chamberpots. Eggcups had to be fashioned from newspaper.

Laura Jewill Hill, later to become a head mistress herself, recalled Miss Bishop telling the staff: 'I have tried to find congenial billets for you. Miss Newman, you will be at the Vicarage – Miss Hill, you will be at the Wellington Arms'.

'I settled happily with the kind landlord and his wife, who provided me with a feather bed, a chop every evening, and the tiny bar-parlour for teaching VIth formers. It showed me what unremitting work it is to run a small pub!'

Her details of everyday life in evacuation mentioned the bitterness of the

Four of the School's Head Mistresses from 1935–1990: (l to r) Barbara Dean, Margaret Gray, Margaret Rudland and Dame Joyce Bishop

Young ladies of the Latymer and Hammersmith Female Charity School – 1840s

The Perfect Dolphin
(rare species)

The Common Dolphin

The Hockey Dolphin
(found on fields and
other boggy places)

Dolphins in uniform – a varied species

90 years on – Godolphin and Latymer staff – 1995 (Courtesy Gillman & Soame, Oxford)

GALUP 'DIY Demo Kit' poster, for march on Parliament – 1975

Misty morning bird's eye view of the new Science/Arts block under construction – 1990 (Courtesy John Stratta)

Exhibition in new Art room, 1995

Hockey and Tennis on the field

Rowing on the Thames above Hammersmith Bridge – 1995

Roll Up! Roll Up! at the Lyric, Hammersmith, 1995

Science for juniors – and seniors

Fourteen-year-old LVs in the University courtyard at Salamanca

Crema

Zagorsk

Sinai desert

Our oldest exchange with our friends at the Johanneum, Hamburg

hostesses, forced to provide accommodation for 5s (25p) a week or 8s 6d (43½p) to include food and the wages paid for work – strawberry picking at 4d (approx 1½p) per hour for girls and 7d (approx 2¾p) per hour for staff – who were not expected to claim it!

Of the Head Mistress, she wrote:

> To all of us who were with the School during those years, Miss Bishop's buoyant spirit, her courage and warmth gave us in our uprooted state a feeling both of challenge and security, and established a closer companionship than we had ever known in London. As she wrestled with the apathy, timidity and obstructiveness of officialdom, we felt at times that she looked upon these as no less an enemy than Hitler; but her diplomacy and determination triumphed. Amid all her personal worries and discomforts, moving house again and again, long hours of travel, heavy administrative burdens, she always found time to give to the individual staff or girl encouragement and sympathy, and she helped us all to look beyond the anxieties and griefs of the time by showing us, by her example, the consolation that comes from working for a cause in which one believes.

So the School reopened, with the playing-field being used for gym as well as games and the hall having to be shared now between the Music Department and Physical Training. It was a comparatively peaceful period, but not for long. The raids by enemy bombers had tailed off as the course of the war was diverted to the Russian front, but by 1944 a new terror was threatening London and the South-East. The first flying bomb – the V1 – had landed in Chiswick, causing massive devastation, and was followed by other V1 raids in rapid succession, with the giant explosive warheads falling indiscriminately all over the capital. One landed near the District Line by Cambridge Grove, destroying a primary school and shattering the windows in Godolphin as well as knocking slates from the roof and causing some structural damage.

Realism overcame optimism and the School had to close from June to September, but the older girls carried on, taking their State examinations in air raid shelters or diving beneath their desks for safety as the *putt-putt* of the V1 engines spluttered overhead before cutting out beyond the School and falling to create more chaos and destruction.

Despite all this, more than 80 Dolphins volunteered to help bring in the harvest at the height of the war, when every ounce of food grown was needed.

This was no easy option. Moira Holton of the Lower VI, described it in the School Magazine:

> We had to work hard during the day, but the work was most interesting and very varied, ranging from potato-lifting, a monotonous job, to fruit-picking. One day we were presented with an immense cart-horse trailing a

weeding machine, to lead up and down rows of cabbages! Some of the work required skill such as stooking, carting and stacking sheaves of wheat, making a hay rick and cutting thistles with a scythe and these skills had to be acquired.

Other jobs, bean and pea-picking and the most unpopular – beetroot thinning – were merely a question of enduring the bending, but we even grew accustomed to this. Plum-picking was the favourite occupation, partly because it was cool in the orchards and partly because of the spice of danger involved in climbing the very precarious ladders, resting against a few twigs with a basket strapped round the waist.... Many were unused to the strange hours we kept, rising at 6.15 a.m. and going to bed at 9 p.m., but we were only too pleased to go to bed early after a tiring day.

Although the V1s were followed by the V2 rockets, which dropped silently from the sky and caused even more destruction than their predecessors, the School survived – battered and tattered – to welcome peace in 1945.

For Miss Bishop, the battle was not over. Once more she was roaring into action, scything through acres of red tape as she struggled to fill in the mountain of official forms which were necessary to claim back from the government the cost of rebuilding the gymnasium and repairing the bomb damage to the rest of the School.

Even more important to her was the task of helping the individual girls to settle back with their families and to deal with the stress which the onslaught of war had forced on them. She and the staff devoted a great deal of time to pastoral work – strengthened in 1947 by the formation of the PTA, the Parent–Teacher Association.

8

THE BATTLES OF PEACE

It is not surprising that so remarkable a woman as Joyce Bishop should have extended her field of interest beyond Godolphin and Latymer. Even while she was holding together and organising the two branches of the School in London and Newbury, she was also keeping pace with the new upsurge of feeling in the country which, although in the thick of another exhausting war, still had the heart to launch the Beveridge Scheme for social security and, in 1944, the new Education Act, aimed at providing full and suitable secondary education for all children in Britain when the war was over.

In her foreword to the School Magazine in 1962–63 she looked back to 1945:

> The present, for me, began after the war when we moved into the period of rebuilding – an exciting creative time which has extended until now. First there was the building up again of the life of the School and its standards of scholarship which have soared to such splendid heights. Then the adapting of ourselves to the new dispensation of the 1944 Education Act. Then came the new buildings – the gymnasium, a most glorious achievement to which the whole family of the School contributed so that we could truly claim 'this was built by private enterprise'. There followed in quick succession the changing room, showers, medical room and waiting room so that, at long last, we had a very satisfactory P.E. block. We paused and took breath for a year or two and then it was possible from our endowments plus a 50% grant from the Ministry of Education, to build a new staff room and to give the most distinguished of staffs a beautiful and spacious setting.
>
> Lastly, we turned all our efforts to the building of the new science laboratories and the conversion of the old ones into much-needed rooms for Art, Craft and Music, and the VIth form rooms as well as the creation of the Gryphon Library out of the old Art Room.

(This was made possible by financial help from the Leche Trust through the School's Chairman of Finance, Angus Acworth. It was named 'Gryphon' after his family coat of arms.)

The building of the new Science block had, alas, only been made possible

A Midsummer Night's Dream set against the Head Mistress's house – 1959

by demolishing the Head Mistress's house to provide space and by the sale of the School's property in St James's Street to help fund the project.

For the staff, the wartime years and the postwar period had been particularly difficult. They had faced their own personal and family tragedies with loved ones lost or wounded as the bombs rained on London and the battles of the war moved across Europe and the Middle and Far East. At the same time, they were committed to supporting the girls who had returned from evacuation in Newbury, helping them to adjust into their homes and into a community where the Little School was *in situ* and not particularly anxious to welcome back to home waters a group of Dolphins who were, for the most part, strangers.

Music and Drama played an essential part in uniting the two factions. The School orchestra was being built up again and taking part, along with the choirs, in the London Secondary Schools Festival. Visits to the Saturday morning concerts in London were being resumed. The School choir broadcast folk songs and children's rhymes on the radio for *Childrens' Hour* and joined with other local schools including Latymer Upper and St Paul's Boys' and Girls' in two programmes of works by Gustav Holst, in his memory – sung in the presence of his daughter, Imogen Holst, and their friend, Dr Ralph Vaughan Williams.

But it was, perhaps, the restoration of the traditional school drama through the inspired team of Viner and Titmuss which, above all, restored unity to the Dolphins.

Beryl Viner's skills lay not only in teaching English but in producing plays

School outing to Capel, Surrey – 1952

– she had been on the brink of joining the BBC Drama Department in the early 1940s and only the exigencies of war had prevented this. Instead, she joined the English Department of Godolphin, met Vera Titmuss and realised that with their combined writing and dramatic skills, added to their love of the theatre, they could do a great deal for the School.

Inspired by their enthusiasm (there was a time when they had spent days making and painting scenery, left it under the stage over half-term and returned to find that mice had eaten much of it) the School enjoyed many years of brilliant productions.

There were musicals – *Hiawatha*, Purcell's *Moon* and spectacular Nativity tableaux at Christmas. *The Tree of Life* written by Vera Titmuss, is still talked of by Old Dolphins. And there were play readings and productions, among them *Richard of Bordeaux*, *The Taming of the Shrew* and stage adaptations of Louis McNeice's *Christopher Columbus*; André Obey's *Noah*; Christopher Fry's *Boy with a Cart* and, in his own old school hall, Yeats's *Land of Heart's Desire*.

The original stage was extended and made more flexible by blocks and steps which also allowed for wings, balconies and other stage effects and provided a background for public speaking, debates and verse-speaking competitions in English, French, German, Latin and Greek.

Nor were the staff forgotten – plays and revues were written for them, too, with a particularly star-studded version of *Alice in Wonderland* for the School's Jubilee Birthday Party in 1955.

85

Joyce Bishop and her staff – 1956

Other departments were also back in their stride, and although times were hard and petrol was among the items still strictly rationed, there were many visits – in and out of London. A group from the Upper V and VIth forms made a memorable trip with the Geography Department to suitably educational villages in Sussex, all going – including the staff – by bicycle. It was, apparently, highly successful despite mops in youth hostel beds and a plethora of 'ghosts'.

While all this was happening, and with the backing of her loyal staff, who willingly supported her many commitments to the world outside School, Joyce Bishop was beginning to play a much greater part in the education scene at national level.

Even in evacuation, she had been a driving force, organising a series of group discussions on such topics of intense contemporary interest as Communism, Capitalism, Education, Christian Motives, Truth and Propaganda. On Education, her own principles were in strong support of free secondary education for all children and she welcomed the 1944 Act because it would 'secure for all children a happier childhood and a better start in life'.

Under the suggested new legislation, children would face three stages: primary, secondary and further education. The Ministry of Education would replace the old Board of Education, and Local Education Authorities were to provide 'schools, sufficient in number, character and equipment to afford all pupils the opportunities for education offering such variety of instruction and training as may be desirable in view of their different ages, abilities and aptitudes and for the different periods for which they may be expected to remain at school, including practical instruction and training appropriate to their respective needs'.

What, then, should be the future of Godolphin and Latymer, a wholly independent, fee-paying establishment?

It was up to the Governors to decide how the School should fit into the new and intricate structure but still preserve its own identity and all that was best in its already rich and varied past. Should it join the great caravan of the State schools or should it take a more private and independent path?

In making this momentous decision, they sought the advice of the Head Mistress and acted on her recommendation. She wrote:

After much careful and anxious thought it was decided that the former was the right way, for along it could the School best share in the task of educating a nation.

In 1945 fees were abolished and the Governors applied for Aided Status, which means that when this is finally granted, the Local Education Authority will be responsible for the whole maintenance of the School (apart from those items connected with the kitchen and the dining hall) and for all external repairs. As members of an Aided School, Dolphins will now enjoy all the privileges and bounties which the State can give, and they, in their turn, must show that they have learned from their founders and benefactors some understanding of the responsibility and duty which the enjoyment of such privileges lays upon them.

Each member of this new community of schools has its own function to perform, its own gifts to offer. For us, it is to foster scholarship and sound learning, to follow knowledge like a shooting star and to offer humbly an imaginative understanding of our fellow creatures born of this pursuit of wisdom, a charity that rejoices in the truth. Surely all this must continue to flourish and to gain fresh vitality as we open wider our window of experience and share with all schools the task of educating the nation.

It was a massive step to take. Godolphin would now be free to offer all its places to girls who were intelligent enough to cope with the academic excellence it was offering, totally regardless of their parents' background or income. It would also mean the end of the Preparatory Department – not acceptable within the government's scheme. Christine Parker, who had enjoyed the 'Prep' and continued throughout the School, sent her daughter, Pauline, to Godolphin and returned to teach Mathematics herself for many years. She recalled its friendly and 'cosy' atmosphere. 'The Prep was based in the Head Mistress's house, and I can remember in the winter, we would sometimes sit round the coal fire while the teacher read to us. It was a wonderful way of easing small girls into the big School later on'.

At the same time, the School's Governing Body remained independent and kept hold of the Deeds of the School, its land, its buildings and, if necessary, any future change of course. Within 20 years this was to prove vitally important.

But even as the administrative wheels were turning to finalise voluntary aided status, Miss Bishop was setting off on other campaigns. Since the first wave of girls' schools had opened, women teachers had, almost without exception, been unmarried and, in many schools, marriage meant the end of a career. Joyce Bishop, 'spinster' supreme, would have none of this. (As one former pupil remarked, 'Miss Bishop was Women's Lib long before its time.') As early as 1947 she was appointed to the Working Party set up by the Minister of Education to enquire into the recruitment of married women to the teaching profession and she pursued her crusade with words and action.

'The spinster, so long a familiar figure of society, is on her way out!' she predicted in a succession of speeches at education conferences. 'In ten years she will be a very rare bird, in twenty years she will be almost extinct in the age groups below sixty'. She believed fervently that the future staffing of girls' schools would have to depend on wives and – indeed – mothers, not just as a stopgap but as members of a great profession, welcome in their own right who would add 'colour and humanity' to school life. Nor were these idle words. By 1963, the staff of 40 teachers at Godolphin and Latymer included 15 married women, 9 of them part-time.

Meanwhile, Miss Bishop was serving as Educational Adviser to the Conservative Political Centre and in 1969 was particularly involved with their radical book *Opportunity for Women* which declared that scientific and mathematical training should be more accessible to girls, day release and sandwich courses should be available to them on the same terms as boys and – to the shock of traditionalists – that the quota which kept so many talented young women out of Universities should be abandoned.

If this makes her sound like a roaring feminist, it was not so. Joyce Bishop enjoyed the company of men as much as of women, at committees and conferences, as antagonists or just as stimulating company across a dinner table – particularly at her house in Malbrook Road, Putney (where her devoted housekeeper, Elizabeth Ellett, was the architect of an endless succession of gourmet dinners superbly cooked and presented by candlelight on a mirror-surfaced table). She particularly enjoyed meeting the husbands and families of Old Dolphins ('but', wrote one OD, 'a husband forfeits her approval if he expects his wife to abandon her career!').

Nor were her battles for women only. She took part in the campaign to modernise entrance procedures at Universities and was welcomed as a member of the University Grants Committee between 1961 and 1963. Her crusading zeal shone as a member of the TV Research Committee, as a UK delegate to UNESCO conferences at Geneva and Montevideo, as a member of the Governing bodies of the Froebel Educational Institute, the National Froebel Foundation and the Royal Ballet Schools and as a member of the Council of Royal Holloway College. She also fitted in the posts of Chairman of the London Aided Schools Association, Chairman of the Joint Four Secondary Associations Committee and membership of the Council for Professions Supplementary to Medicine.

In 1950 the Governors of Godolphin decided that she deserved sabbatical leave not because she was in any way flagging in her dedication to so many causes and particularly the School, but more as a tribute to her brilliance. Diplomatically, as the statutes demanded, they 'sought permission' from the Education Officer – but with the words 'you will be delighted to hear that Miss Bishop has agreed to take a sabbatical term'.

It was, she always said, the most wonderful holiday of her life, travelling by air, coach, car, Jeep, limousine and camel from Syracuse to Cairo. Throughout the journey she wrote constantly to the School, much as a mother might keep in touch with her family, enthusing over the travelling ('I enjoyed every moment of the flight...I much enjoyed the barley sugar I was given to suck when we were climbing – I chose it rather than chewing gum; you will have heard about the 14 hours train journey – at intervals a man came in with a feather brush to dust us and the carriage.... At Luxor, Aboudi the guide turned up. We were very lucky to get him because he now only conducts the chosen few; his father was guide to my aunt over 40 years ago! He won't take Americans because they make too much noise and ask too many questions.... We approached the Temple of Amun Ra along the avenue of Ram-headed Sphinxes. I suppose they are all the same but I thought they had different expressions and I didn't like the look in the eyes of some of them at all!' And, anxiously, 'Do tell me if every Form has received at least one card from me. I am a little worried as to whether some I sent from Egypt ever arrived'.)

While Miss Bishop was in Kyrenia, news came through that she had been elected President of the Association of Head Mistresses – the professional body concerned with educational problems, particularly in grammar schools for girls. The brilliance of her term of office was recognised officially in 1953 when she was created C.B.E. and, unofficially, in *The Times Educational Supplement*, which described her as 'an able, gracious and witty president of the HMA'.

Her retirement as Head Mistress in 1963 marked the end of a period which had built up the reputation and achievements of Godolphin and Latymer not only within its own walls but as reflecting the rapid changes which were taking place throughout Britain and the world as a whole.

When Miss Bishop and Woggs walked into Iffley Road in 1935, wireless was in its infancy, television was scarcely heard of, air travel was for the wealthy few, cinemas with 'talking pictures' were spreading fast, very few mothers – other than the poorest or, occasionally, the wealthiest – went out to work and children were still, for the most part, seen and not heard. She had led the School into the first-ever evacuation from the threat of enemy bombing and kept it going throughout the greatest world war in history, emerging into an era when the 'lower classes' were in near revolt and equality, with social security for all, from the cradle to the grave, was being fostered by the government as a right. Few homes were without radio and many already had television sets. Air travel, transformed by wartime research, was becoming commonplace. The atom bomb had fallen and mushroomed into a worldwide searching of conscience over the morality of such a weapon and the whole future of nuclear energy. Already, the 'earthquake' era for British education was starting and the comprehensive schools movement was under way.

In leaving, Dame Joyce Bishop wrote: 'I want you to see all that I have done in the context of a great school – without it and all that it meant to me, I should have done nothing. The excellence of schools like this must be allowed to survive whatever else emerges from the chaos of re-organisation of secondary education'.

9

SAVING GODOLPHIN

From the many applicants for the post of Head Mistress of Godolphin and Latymer the Governors chose the one person who could, above all, not only follow successfully in the footsteps of Dame Joyce Bishop, but who had the character, personality and experience to face and deal with the turmoil which lay ahead as education plunged into a world of incoherently changing patterns. Almost overnight, it seemed, the young had adopted the American title of 'teenagers' and rocketed via Beatlemania, pop music and rock and roll into an era exemplified by one much vaunted best-selling group, which declared, openly and with all too much popular acclaim – 'We don't need no ejucashun'.

It was greatly due to Margaret Gray's friendly and cheerful personality and her ability to tolerate much that was modern and acceptable while putting a firm foot down on what was 'over the top' and inadmissible, that Godolphin managed to steer a steady course through the stormy 1960s and '70s.

Margaret Caroline Gray was the youngest child of the Rev. Dr Herbert Gray, a distinguished Minister of the Presbyterian Church, an army chaplain from the First World War who (as was mentioned in an earlier chapter) became a pacifist involved with the founding of the Peace Pledge Union. Added to this, he had been a left-wing 'parson' in the slums of Glasgow and Manchester and author of a book on sex and religion, *Men, Women and God*, which had caused a furore when it was published in the 1920s, became a best seller and was largely responsible for his founding the Marriage Guidance Council. His wife, Margaret's mother, was the daughter of Principal Marcus Dods of the New College, Edinburgh, a biblical scholar who had the distinction of standing trial for challenging the fundamentalist view of the verbal inspiration of the Bible, in the last heresy case in Scotland.

Although Margaret was born in Glasgow and started her school life there, she moved with her family when her father came to London to take over a campaign of social work among the needy in the slums of the East End. Because of this she was, herself, all too well aware of and sympathetic to the problems and the hardships of the poor. She was educated at St Mary's Hall, Brighton, and read History at Newnham College, Cambridge, before spending a postgraduate fellowship year in the USA at Smith College.

In 1995, sitting in her warm, sunny flat at the top of the house in Kew,

Margaret Gray

which, for the many years of her retirement she shared with Vera Titmuss and Beryl Viner, both of whom had been Deputy Head Mistresses at Godolphin, she recalled her time in the School.

'I came to G & L in September 1963 after 11 years as Head of another voluntary aided London grammar school, the Skinners' Company's School for Girls at Stamford Hill in the Borough of Hackney. Before that, I had been evacuated with the Mary Datchelor School, Camberwell, so that though I had been very happy at Skinners', coming to G & L was like coming home. Both the Datchelor and Godolphin had highly distinguished but also human Head Mistresses – Dame Dorothy Brock and Dame Joyce Bishop – who were friends and shared the same pioneering and enlightened view of girls' education. Both schools had outstanding staffs, headed by people of tremendous calibre, skill and humanity such as Vera Titmuss, Miss Scott, Miss Samways, Miss Dean, Miss Alma Mathews, Miss Gabriel and many others. Both had a lifelong reputation for fine music and brilliant drama departments. Both did a lot of social service, both were full of extremely articulate and immensely varied girls, not all turned out to a pattern but mostly headed in the direction of further education, so both had large and lively VIth forms.

'I immediately liked, admired and felt at ease in G & L and had no desire to make a lot of changes – I wanted to see what made a great school tick so cheerfully and effectively.

'But, of course, it was 1963 and, largely unperceived at first, forces were at work in society which London girls had to cope with or succumb. Before long we were having to face the problem of drugs, of the decreasing safety of the streets, of the occasional unwanted pregnancy and of the near-suicide of a particularly brilliant girl in the period between her Oxford and Cambridge scholarship exams.

'Despite all the distractions, excellent work went on being done; G & L took leading parts in inter-school debating, in the work of the Red Cross, in the welfare of the old, in the Council for Education in World Citizenship (an organisation which had been set up soon after the Second World War as a junior branch of the United Nations Association); in the inter-school Student Christian Movement; in inter-school verse-speaking competitions and in its own internal drama and piano competitions and its lovely Christmas Carol Concerts.

'With huge enthusiasm every July the School held a fête which raised vast sums of money for the Francha Leal Fund, which was, and is, administered by the Head Mistress for the quiet, inconspicuous but immensely appreciated help of past and present Dolphins in financial hardship. From providing games equipment for a girl whose family couldn't afford it to helping with the training or retraining of Old Dolphins, it was a timely help to many people. It also sowed the seed which bore such fruit later in the Bursary Fund, that a School like G & L should, as far as it possibly could, raise money to help itself rather than rely solely on outside grants. And these were the days when many Dolphin families knew real poverty, were having free school meals, needing uniform grants and, in the case of the Upper VIth and VIIth, needing help to find the fares to attend University interviews.

'In my fourth term, the autumn of 1964, the School was subjected to a

Ministry of Education Inspection (Dame Joyce had always said she was too busy – and had got away with it!). In those days this meant a week when a team of HM Inspectors descended on the School, attended lessons, examined the buildings and the administration and wrote a detailed report at the end. It was something of a strain, but we had a good team and their leader confided at the end of the week that the Inspectors had said "This is the best grammar school we have ever visited".

The cloisters were glazed in 1971

'In those early years too, the Science Department, led by Miss Marjorie Gordon and then Miss Frances Eastwood (who later became Chairman of the Association for Science Education), was pioneering, in company with a few other leading schools such as Eton, the development of Nuffield Physics and Nuffield Chemistry. This demanded that every girl carried out her own experiments, and therefore entailed the acquiring and storing of a vast amount of new equipment in what was then the new Science Building. But it also meant that our Science staff were in touch with pioneers in the teaching of Science and that brushed off on the girls and contributed to the fact that Dolphins were not in the least intimidated by Science and felt none of the inhibitions about Physics and Chemistry which were unfortunately felt in some other girls' and co-ed schools.

'Another thing which greatly impressed and delighted me was that, apart from the Upper Vth and Upper VIth facing O Level and A Level, School examinations were not marked in marks out of a hundred but only graded, which made it impossible to make form mark lists. No one could be seen to be "top" and, even more importantly – no one could be seen to be "bottom".

Margaret Lovell's sculpture *Barquentine III* in the paved courtyard

Despite this, many Old Dolphins will confirm with a chuckle that there was often a clandestine movement within many forms to work out their pecking order – whatever the ethical or psychological rights or wrongs. It was, however, an excellent plan and led to one of the changes which was introduced early in Miss Gray's time – abolition of the system of having an 'a' form and an 'x' and 'y' form in each year. Instead, girls were divided arbitrarily when they arrived and their forms identified by the initial of their form mistress. After the first year they were divided into four groups for French and Mathematics (both subjects in which, as she explained 'it is agony to be pushed too fast or held back too slowly'), but went straight on as forms for all other subjects. This was, she said, a good system which by no means

Champions – the hockey team – 1959–60

deprived girls of incentives to do well, but removed the over-importance of being 'top'.

Uniform, which early Dolphins had been proud to wear, was now becoming a sore point and a matter for controversy. Miss Gray went on: 'When I came, the VIth form wore grey skirts of any pattern and coloured jerseys of their own choosing. We fairly soon abolished all restriction on VIth form clothes, simply saying "please remember that you are dressing for work, not for the beach or the dance hall". Although this led to protests by some parents who had to endure the daily agony of "what can I wear today?" it was largely welcomed'. The rest of the School wore grey skirts with deep turquoise blouses and grey cardigans or sweaters plus, of course, grey blazers with the school badge on the pocket. A grey beret had taken the place of the former felt or panama hat but never caught on and was seldom seen. In Miss Gray's time, the outer garment became a grey overcoat or, later, a then-fashionable grey duffel coat with a scarlet-lined hood. Even so, the manner in which it was worn tended to vary according to age, from the impeccable UIIIs to some less amenable older Dolphins.

'There was less foreign travel than now – purely for financial reasons – but there were ILEA Travelling Scholarships, a German exchange with the Johanneum in Hamburg and there were pen-friends which led to inter-family exchanges. Many members of the VIIth form (who stayed on an extra term to take the Oxbridge entrance examinations and interviews) managed to get abroad during the nine months between school and college, sometimes helped by the Elizabeth Godolphin Fund. After Mrs Jean Prynne joined the

The 'new' Science block on the site of the former Head Mistress's House

staff, there were two expeditions to the Soviet Union, long before most schools in the West had the opportunity to make the journey behind the Iron Curtain. Increasingly, after Miss Berenice Goodwin arrived, we had Art and Art History visits to Italy and, later, France and Holland.

'Drama was always very strong at G & L. My first School play was *Twelfth Night* in 1964, produced by Mrs Talbot. The standard was uniformly high, the cast brilliant with perhaps a touch of genius in Judith Coleman, the Head Girl, as Sir Andrew – the funniest I have ever seen on or off the professional stage; the appearance elegant and charming, the whole highly polished. Another highlight of 1966 was *Noye's Fludde*, jointly and delightfully produced by the English and Music Departments and involving large numbers of the School, of all ages.

'When Miss Goodwin produced School plays, they involved rather fewer girls because she used boys from Latymer Upper, St Paul's and other schools in the male parts. The productions reached a very high standard indeed and were often performed "in the round" in the Cockpit Theatre off Edgware Road.

'Also, as many Old Dolphins will remember with joy, there were the hilarious staff plays on every School Birthday – miracles of invention, improvisation, dramatic skill and produced with maximum success and minimum rehearsing and always rapturously received by the School. We always maintained the tradition of singing the School Song, which went back to 1913, although Vera Titmuss updated it to fit in more suitably to life at

Iffley Road in the 1960s.

'The buildings were good, but there were needs. The School Office was a tiny room beneath the stairs at the far end of the lower corridor (later to become the Deputy Head's study) and was so small for three people that we were told it would be condemned in any factory! So we sacrificed a classroom on the ground floor and made it into the present office.

'When I came, the telephone system was operated from the Head Mistress's study on an antique machine with a wind-up handle. Much as I admired Dame Joyce, I could not stomach that, so a more modern system, centred in the office, was established. There was no VIth form common room and no staff dining room.

'Gradually, with the co-operation of the ILEA, these deficiencies were remedied, but in order to adapt you had to keep within the cost of a "minor improvement" – i.e. you had a price ceiling of £25,000. In spite of that, we managed to demolish an old building at the end of the cloister and build an extension [now superseded] for a large VIth form common room, several Music rooms, an Art room and three VIth form rooms. The cloister was enclosed, the courtyard paved and a raised rose garden with its sculpture were introduced and, at the same time, rose beds were planted to flank the newly laid drive on the "garden front" of the School.

'Not all of this was paid for by the ILEA. As a voluntary aided school, the Governors could use, if they so willed, the interest of the School's endow-

'The funniest Sir Andrew ever ...' *Twelfth Night* – 1964

ment – in our case £60,000 – which originated from the sale of the School's property in St James's Street.

'At that time we had an extremely interesting, artistic (and a mite dictatorial!) Chairman of the Finance Committee called Angus Acworth, who was also Chairman of the Georgian Society. He wanted to improve the appearance of the School, and under his guidance and to our huge relief, the depressing, cracked white 'public lavatory' tiles which clothed the walls of the lower and upper corridors were covered by the present warm, pleasant panelling. He also sponsored the paving of the courtyard and the improvement of the front garden, the rose garden and some of the trees.

'Angus Acworth also asked me what I most wanted to spend money on. Apart from the panelling in the corridors, my first choice was sabbatical terms for the senior staff, which were duly started – Miss Eastwood had the first in 1968.

'Apart from this, he also sponsored a fund for buying contemporary works of art for the school. This money, from the sale of the houses which the niece of Sir William Godolphin had bought for the charity after his death, was named after her, the Elizabeth Godolphin Fund, and it was also used to help fund foreign travel and school expeditions.

'But my most abiding memory of my ten and a half years at G & L is of the quality and friendship of the staff. Dame Joyce was a wonderful appointer and she left me a staff of highly qualified, very individual and most distinguished women, all approachable – none lofty. When some of my colleagues in the Association of Head Mistresses let their hair down about difficult staff, I felt almost embarrassed because it would have seemed smug to say "I don't have those problems" – but I didn't. Of course, there were some difficulties – it would have been highly unnatural otherwise – but they were not deeply divisive and they didn't upset the ethos of the School which was purposeful, hardworking, effective and, in teaching, highly skilled but also friendly, relaxed and cheerful. The staff room lobby was always full of girls talking to teachers about every sort of problem – mainly to do with work but also personal problems too – it was a tradition which went back to the earliest days.

'During my time there, the centre of this feeling in the School was Vera Titmuss. Quietly and always without fuss, she radiated a deeply sympathetic attitude in the staff room. A wonderful teacher of English, she never imposed her personal methods on her department but left them free to develop their own individual gifts and was the perfect bridge between staff room and Head's room and, for me, the chief interpreter of the School's character.

'But there were many others too, including Ruth Walsh, the School Secretary, whose phenomenal memory and lifetime in the School (she had joined as a junior and spent her whole school life there before returning to become Secretary) was beyond rubies. Vera Titmuss, with Barbara Dean and Miss Scott were form mistresses of the UVI and VIIth and not only wrote

99

wonderfully perceptive UCCA forms about their girls but created a tremendous feeling of friendly co-operation and respect for good scholarship which made a splendid jumping-off ground for University life and work.

'The VIIth form was especially valuable. This was a term totally free of school offices, preparing in small groups for Oxbridge scholarship examinations, which were then very demanding, followed by eight to nine months of freedom to travel, work or just grow up before coping with University life.

'Barbara Rowe and Betty Kershaw led a distinguished Modern Language Department in which Mrs Beckett taught Spanish and Mrs Knuppfer Russian – her native tongue. Mrs Beckett also ran the Secretarial VIth, and her standards there, too, were extremely high. She didn't just teach shorthand, typing and bookkeeping but how to behave and dress, down to meticulous details such as the care of fingernails! Many of her girls combined Secretarial Studies with one or two A Levels and got good posts with ease as soon as they left School, which often led to the most enterprising careers.

'The other outstanding good fortune I had at G & L was my Chairman of Governors, Lady Brooke – always a warm, well-informed and experienced support – who became a great friend. Staff, parents, girls and I could all rely on her for sympathy, wise advice, shrewd knowledge of the world and a very real commitment to the School'.

Following the principle embodied most notably in Dame Joyce that the Head of Godolphin had something to offer to the larger world of education,

Lady Brooke, Chairman of Governors, helped the School to survive and was first Chairman of the Bursary Fund

Margaret Gray was, for two years, Chairman of the London Joint 4 and from 1970–72 Chairman of the Committee of the Association of Head Mistresses, although she refused to be nominated as President because she wanted to spend her final 18 months at G & L actually in the School. She was also Chairman of the National Advisory Centre on Careers for Women from 1970–92. (Founded in 1933 it was the pioneer and for many years the only careers advisory body for women and girls.)

Meanwhile, outside the School, this was a period of unrest. The nation was assured that it had 'never had it so good', but there were many people who were shocked and bewildered by the shadow of the atom bomb, and just as the Dolphins of the 1930s had been deeply concerned with peace movements, so had many of their successors become involved with such organisations as CND – the Campaign for Nuclear Disarmament – joining in huge, protest marches.

In education, too, there were increasing problems. Those who, at the time of the 1944 Education Act, were looking to a more drastic solution than it eventually provided were still pressing for an end to selective schools, for all State schools in Britain to become comprehensive and to accept all children to develop to the maximum whatever talent they had – academic or otherwise.

In theory it was appealing; in practice, and timed at the moment when the old-fashioned theories of family, religion, loyalty and discipline were breaking down and the cult of commercial exploitation of the teenager was burgeoning, the imposition of huge schools with inadequate discipline could not have arrived at a worse moment.

The first alarm bells sounded for Godolphin and Latymer in 1966 when the ILEA suggested a scheme to the Governors for a 'small comprehensive' on the Iffley Road site which would have involved building across the entire playing-field. The Governors studied the scheme and turned it down on the grounds that they 'did not think the proposed new school could make a better contribution to the education of London's children than the present school could make'.

For four years there was uneasy silence, then, in 1970, Margaret Gray, the Chairman of Governors, Lady Brooke of Cumnor, and the Deputy Head, Barbara Dean, were summoned by Dr Eric Briault, ILEA's Chief Education Officer, to a meeting of Heads of Secondary Schools in Division One – West London.

On arriving, they were shown a map of schools which would lose their identity under the Labour-controlled council's new plans for complete comprehensivisation. To their astonishment – and horror – Godolphin and Latymer had been obliterated under a large black cross.

During the course of the next few hours they were left in no doubt that ILEA was planning to destroy all London's grammar schools. Some comprehensives were already in being, purpose-built to high specification in comfortable areas of London – the prestigious Holland Park in Kensington and Crown Woods in Eltham were two of the earliest. But the money would not stretch to provide the splendour of these trail-blazers for every area, so for many of the rest, it was a question of joining with other schools in their area and making the best of what already existed.

The scheme for Godolphin and Latymer would have linked it with St Clement Dane's and Burlington School, both a mile or more away from Iffley Road along busy roads at the edge of Wormwood Scrubs. For some lessons, pupils would be expected to commute between all three buildings.

The news was broken to the staff and letters were sent to parents explaining the scheme.

The result was uproar. A meeting was called to discuss the prospect and the response from parents was so great that the proceedings in the School hall had to be relayed to an even larger group in the gym. As a result of what they heard, they decided to form their own Association, which could, if necessary, face ILEA free from any of the inhibitions which might restrict the Governors and staff for whom ILEA was in the position of employer.

While the teachers and Governors made their own plans, the parents set up GALUP – the Godolphin and Latymer Union of Parents. Chaired by the then Secretary of the PTA, Sally Holloway, its organising committee included Sir Peter Henderson (later Lord Henderson), James Macnair, George Nissen and Peter Sherwood – all of whom became Governors of the School later. Its Secretary was Gerald O'Brien, who, with four daughters in or hoping to enter the School, was determined to do all he could to help maintain its high standards. He worked with dedication and skill, and everyone grieved when soon after the campaign ended, he died of cancer. But all his daughters became Dolphins.

The call to make the School a comprehensive was not turned down out of hand. The Governors and teachers studied the scheme in depth and GALUP organised a series of subcommittees to discuss the way in which the School might comply with the Authority's demands without lowering standards, as well as ways in which, if the crunch came, it might revert to its original fee-paying independent status.

Leading it all was Lady Brooke, Chairman of the Governors, a Baroness in her own right and wife of Lord Brooke, a former Home Secretary. Her knowledge of politics was outstanding, but added to this, she was fair-minded and concerned to carry out the will of the rest of the Governing Body, the teachers and the parents.

Among these, there was a small core who believed that the School should go along with the ILEA plan, but the overwhelming majority were concerned, above all, with maintaining the tradition of high standards.

The first scheme was eventually withdrawn, but in its place, ILEA decided that Godolphin should form a smaller comprehensive, 'twinned' with Mary Boon, an excellent school close to Olympia which specialised in catering and upholstery. Once more, pupils would be expected to commute between the two buildings – a journey which would involve walking through some of London's busiest streets as well as crossing Hammersmith Broadway with its seething traffic.

Throughout the first half of the 1970s, the battle for Godolphin and Latymer went on as almost all the threatened London grammar schools came together to save themselves. Many failed to survive, but Godolphin had one great strength. When negotiations had been in hand before the School opted for voluntary aided status, Dame Joyce Bishop and Dame Dorothy Brock had toured the independent grammar schools of London, warning them to look carefully at the agreement they were being offered. It was, they stressed, essential that the independent Governors should maintain their majority on the Governing Body and not hand over power to the politicians. Not all schools were able to do this, and those who could not were the ones which foundered in this strife. Thanks to Dame Joyce Bishop and Lady Moberly, who had been Chairman of Governors at the time, Godolphin and Latymer had accepted one-third of its Governors as political appointees but had insisted on maintaining the remaining two-thirds as independents, including those representing the Godolphin family, the Latymer Foundation and the University of London. It still owned its buildings and its site in Iffley Road, so it was in a position to dictate its own future rather than give way to the demands of the Education Authority.

Throughout this time, the School's parents monitored all the Education Committee Meetings at County Hall, Westminster, and reported back to the Governors and staff. The teachers, led by Miss Gray and, later, Miss Dean, with much hard work by Mrs Ena Mason, spent a great deal of time in producing a detailed document suggesting ways in which the School might, within the limits of the grant being offered for the change, become a comprehensive on its own site. But whatever happened, they insisted that they would accept no scheme which reduced the School's traditional high standards.

By 1973 most of London's grammar schools had closed ranks in opposition to ILEA's plans and for the time being there was a lull in the battle. It seemed that there might, indeed, be no further threat to the School. Accordingly, Margaret Gray, who had reached her sixtieth birthday, decided to retire. It was a sad day for Dolphins, who bade farewell to the much-loved Head who had steered them with great skill, love and understanding through the early days of the teenage revolution and the first skirmishes in what was, alas, with a suddenly changed political situation, all too soon to become a battle for survival.

On her last day, after weeks of whispering and secretive meetings by girls in odd corners, she was given a magnificent send-off. The Old Dolphins had already given her a large collection of assorted gifts. The PTA had presented her with a Georgian mahogany bureau. Now, the whole School had signed a ten-feet-long scroll, complete with wax seal and, along with it, had given their retiring Head a present they were convinced she would continue to use for many years. They were, of course, right. To cheers from them all, she wobbled briefly with emotion and the state of the front drive before heading for retirement with a large smile, pedalling furiously on a brand new bicycle.

It was to be by no means her final appearance at Iffley Road.

10

A MATTER OF LIFE OR DEATH

Rather than risk bringing in a new figure with little understanding of all that G & L stood for at what might still be a vital stage in the School's existence, the Governors opted for a candidate who knew the ethos better than most.

Understandably, every girl had watched apprehensively as strange applicants had been conducted round the classrooms during the preliminary stages of selection, and there was tension in Assembly as, at last, the name of her successor was announced by Margaret Gray herself.

It would, she said, be Barbara Dean, already the Deputy Head. Before she could say any more her words were drowned by the roar of cheers and the traditional thunderous stamping of feet, which shook the hall from floor to rafters. There was no doubt that this was a popular appointment of a much-loved teacher.

Barbara Dean had been educated at North London Collegiate School, where she had been Senior Prefect before going to Cambridge and then taking a teaching post at Roedean. She stayed there for a short period before returning to her parents' home in West London and joining the History Department of Godolphin and Latymer. Quiet and shy, she was a brilliant teacher and organiser and had a deep understanding of the girls she taught. Surprisingly, she also had a reputation for her scintillating and totally out of character performances in the Staff Revue on the School Birthday each year.

Within months of taking over, she was plunged into the full battle for the life of the School.

Soon after Margaret Gray's retirement, the whole question of abolishing London's grammar schools had flared up again, dominating much of Barbara Dean's earliest period of Headship. The battle reached a peak of intensity in 1975 when more than 1,000 parents representing almost all the 700 girls in Godolphin and Latymer attended a meeting so large that the banqueting hall at the new Cunard (later the Novotel) Hotel off Hammersmith Broadway had to be booked – and was packed to the doors. The views of those who were in favour of the comprehensive scheme and those against were heard, but a huge majority demanded that the School should stay as it was – a selective grammar school, maintaining its traditional high standards within the State system.

Plans were made to back this up with a protest march, and GALUP pro-

Barbara Dean

duced a 'DIY Demo Kit' – a poster which combined a dolphin banner for the march, plus stickers for car windscreens, satchels or lapels, all blazoned with the call 'Save Godolphin and Latymer'. Carrying the cut-out dolphins on poles – and with prior permission from the remarkably co-operative and sympathetic Metropolitan Police – the parents marched on Parliament. This was, they argued, a school which had always welcomed girls from any background – its present parents ranged from a cabinet maker to a Cabinet Minister – and it was too valuable to be destroyed.

'A deep understanding of the girls she taught'

106

It was to no avail. After reading the detailed reports submitted by Governors, staff and parents of the School, the Chairman of the Education Committee of ILEA met the deputation from Godolphin one more time at County Hall. It was a memorable occasion. The Committee had, she explained, read all that had been said about the School. They accepted the claim that if the Governors agreed to the Authority's plans the standard of education would fall for all future pupils whatever their ability, but, she stressed, 'you must realise that in our Labour Party Manifesto we said that we would make London fully comprehensive and this is the policy which we intend to carry out'.

By now, they had decided that Godolphin and Latymer was, in any case, too small a unit to keep in their system, and it would, accordingly, be phased out and closed by 1982.

Outside the chilly panelled committee room, a tug on the Thames hooted mournfully on the high tide as the Godolphin deputation made its way out into the warm sunlight of Westminster Bridge. Angry and dazed, they walked silently across to the District Line station. The GALUP subcommittee which had looked into the possibility of taking the School back into independence had warned that it would not be an easy road. On the other hand, if it stayed in the State system it would be closed anyway.

By the end of the journey back to Hammersmith, Lady Brooke was courageously clear in her mind what the course must be. After a last consultation with the staff, parents and her fellow Governors, she made the announcement. From September 1977, Godolphin and Latymer would return to its original fee-paying status as an independent school.

In taking this decision, Godolphin and Latymer became the only voluntary aided girls' school in London to opt for independence — and all the problems it would entail, not least the structure for entrance examinations but, above all, for the administration, most of which had been the responsibility of the local authority for so many years.

Latymer Upper had been a Direct Grant school, which meant that it had kept its fee-paying basis but took in many pupils who were supported by the local authority. Now it, too, had to reorganise, and in doing this, the two schools began to link more closely than they had in the past. Soon they were sharing a Clerk to the Governors and some of the maintenance staff — among them John Stratta.

Since its earliest days, Godolphin had been blessed with loyal and memorable schoolkeepers, including the famous Mr Atkins of the WW2 period and later, Mr 'Bob' Tayler and his collie dog Laddie, all of whom had cared devotedly for the School and everything it stood for. When Mr Tayler retired, his place was taken by John Stratta, and once more the lodge by the School gates was occupied not only by a most professional, skilful 'keeper' but by his wife Lorna and his family, Ian, Gary and Sara, who loyally supported the School in its fund-raising events and became an integral part of

From the first Bursary Fund brochure in 1977 – appealing Dolphins with Laddie, Schoolkeeper Bob Tayler's dog

the Godolphin and Latymer family.

Above all, now the cost of running the School fell on the Governors. Economically viable fees had to be set – and staff appointed to handle them. Entrance examinations needed to be organised, prospective parents welcomed and shown round the building. All this was accomplished with a minimum of fuss – so little, in fact, that few of the pupils realised that there had been any change. Those who were in the School already still had their fees paid for by ILEA, but each first year became fee-paying until eventually the whole school was back in full independence.

Many of the people who had fought for the School over those previous five years were particularly concerned now for its traditional social mixture and were absolutely determined that this must not be lost. Accordingly, the Bursary Fund was launched to help pay part if not all the fees for bright girls whose parents would not be able to afford them. Leading it, as Chairman, Margaret Gray returned from retirement, and with customary cheerful enthusiasm took over the hard work of raising £500,000 to prime the Fund.

It was soon clear that she too would need more secretarial help than the School Office could manage, and once more, Godolphin had the good fortune to discover Mrs Gill Capel, who not only helped in the campaign – which, indeed, raised its half million – but stayed on and retrained to become the School Bursar.

Some of the money raised came through the generosity of a number of big and sympathetic companies, particularly British Oxygen, then based at Hammersmith, which also provided specialist help and whose Chairman, Sir Leslie Smith, became a member of the Bursary Committee. A sponsored walk 'round the bridges' (from Hammersmith along the towpath to Chiswick and back through Mortlake and Barnes to cross Hammersmith Bridge and return to Iffley Road) raised more than £5,000, much of it through the determination of Sir Nicholas Goodison and his wife Judith, who was, by now, a Governor of the School. They not only covered the distance but Sir Nicholas, then Chairman of the Stock Exchange, roared round the course with extra verve, explaining that he had been sponsored by many of his colleagues with a bonus for every girl he overtook.

But much of the money came from the efforts of the girls themselves, who organised a string of fund-raising events.

One of the first Bursaries to be offered by the Fund was the result of money collected mainly by Old Dolphins in honour of the eightieth birthday of Dame Joyce Bishop – and was named after her.

Even with the value of money then, the School would have been hard pressed to take in all the girls they would have wished with the £500,000 but in September 1981, an Assisted Places Scheme was launched by the government to help parents who had difficulty in paying fees for academically bright daughters. This had an upper limit, and parents whose income was close to it received a minimal grant, ranging down to some whose income

109

was so small that they paid no fees and were helped with uniform and other expenses. Godolphin took the maximum AP places available – 35 at 11 + and 5 for VIth form entrants.

Once more the School enjoyed its traditional mixed social background and, briefly, the immediate pressure was lifted from the Bursary Fund – but not for long. The recession of the late 1980s and early 1990s, when many parents who had thought they were in safe employment for life found themselves suddenly made redundant, hit hard and the Bursary Fund responded to an unprecedented number of calls for help to keep girls in the School. Without its help, they might not have been able to stay. Many of the luckier parents who were able to find new employment repaid the money which the fund had provided in the hope that it might help someone else. For the less fortunate ones, there was no hope of this and the Fund had to continue raising money as best it could to make up its dwindling resources.

In fact, the anxieties of those who had wondered whether the School would survive the changed status were soon swept away. Far from falling numbers, Godolphin and Latymer was clearly thriving as candidates flocked to register for the entrance examination at 11 + and for the VIth form entry tests.

Throughout its existence the girls' school, unlike the unlucky boys' school which had preceded it, had been fortunate in its Governors and its Chairmen of Governors. Thomas Chamberlen, The Bishop of Worcester, J Glasier, Sir William Bull (whose son George was also a long-serving Governor) and Sir Marshall Hays had all served loyally and conscientiously. In 1948, Sir Marshall Hays had died suddenly while he was still in office. Lady Moberly, who was already a Governor and was a close friend of Miss Bishop, was asked to take his place, and for the first time in its history, the School had a woman Chairman. Lady Moberly served with great success until 1961, when her place was taken by Lady Brooke. Barbara Brooke too served with loyalty and skill for 17 years, and without her firm and dedicated leadership during the battle for its life, Godolphin and Latymer might not have continued to exist.

By 1978 she felt that she could no longer give the School the time and energy she had in the past, so, with great regret, the Governors accepted her resignation. After a party given by the staff and parents at Christmas 1978, her place was taken by another governor, Janet Glover, C.B.E., M.A.

Janet Glover had retired from the Headship of Sutton High School in 1973 and had been President of the Head Mistresses' Association. As Chairman she was leading a School which was firmly back on its feet and looking to the future. The need now was for consolidation and expansion.

Ironically, it was in 1982, the year in which the School would have been closed had it stayed in the maintained sector, that the Governors agreed on a major building scheme.

More rooms were needed, particularly for the smaller teaching groups of

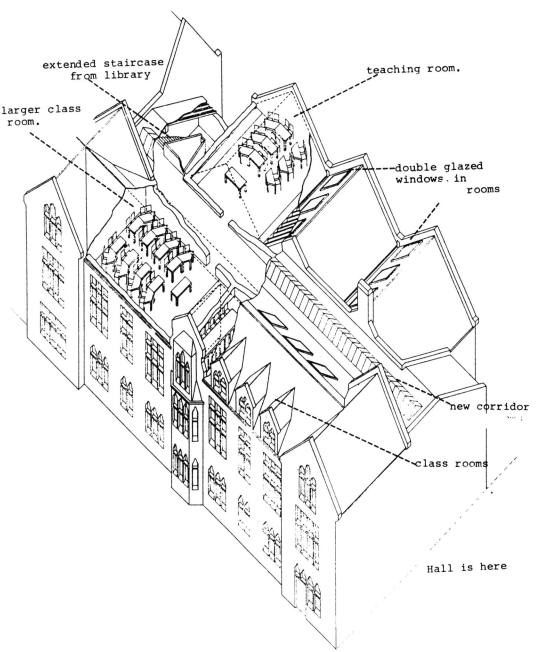

extended staircase
from library

teaching room.

larger class
room.

double glazed
windows. in
rooms

new corridor

class rooms

Hall is here

Architect Hans Haenlein's axonometric view of the roof conversion – completed in 1984 (Courtesy Hans Haenlein Associates)

seniors studying subjects like Spanish and Russian as well as for improved Careers advice. Space in the School building was at a premium. Every inch was inspected in the hope of finding somewhere suitable. It was a Hammersmith-based architect with an international reputation, Hans Haenlein, who hit on the idea of opening up the old attics of the Victorian building. In the earliest days these had been the servants' bedrooms and the sick bay of the boys' school. Later, the floors had been raised to provide loftier rooms on the first floor.

As School broke up for the summer holidays of 1983, the builders moved in to corset the old building in scaffolding front and back and literally to raise the roof. A vast false roof of corrugated iron (which rumbled like stage thunder in high winds) was erected over the main building and the slates were removed. The floors of the attic rooms, which provided the ceilings for the first floor, were completely drilled and hacked away, then lowered slightly, and the new top corridor was built, airy and light with windows to the sky. Opening from each side were new classrooms, a language laboratory and, at the western end, a resources room where the School's printing could be produced with more modern equipment than the old-fashioned duplicating machine or its even earlier counterpart – the tray of jelly with purple ink.

Hopes that it might be finished by Christmas were more than optimistic. The autumn term had opened to the crash of plaster as it cascaded down into skips on the drive. (And, on one memorable afternoon, on a French class of juniors after their ceiling collapsed under the strain of so much vibration. A line of small, grey, dust-covered figures filed out, blinking, from the fog of powdered plaster to be checked over, brushed down and, thankfully, declared free of injury.)

It was September 1984 when the Hon. Peter Brooke, Parliamentary Under-Secretary of State at the Department of Education and Science and son of Lady Brooke, climbed the new staircase to the top floor and formally declared the 'outer space' open.

The old Secretarial VIth had, of necessity, breathed its last during Margaret Gray's term as Head, but although the typewriters had gone, computers, which only a short time ago had barely been heard of, were becoming established in the School, thanks initially to a gift of money from a parent who saw the potential of this new form of technology and urged the School to start teaching about them. Another welcome contribution had come from the proceeds of the now-established second-hand uniform sale. Even so, in 1981, computers were still for the use of the VIth form only and for a restricted number of subjects, with the hope that they would be extended to the rest of the School later. They were – rapidly. At about this time, too, the first video recorder was being rented and used to record History, Geography and Religious Education programmes.

An extension to the School Magazine had also been established. New printing techniques, which were already wreaking havoc in the traditional 'hot metal' production of national newspapers, were becoming more readily available to the public. Again with the help of some parents, the School took advantage of this to launch a four-page news-sheet – *The Dolphin* – which could keep staff and pupils in touch with events in other parts of the School and give parents (at least, those whose daughters remembered to take the paper home and hand it over) the opportunity to discover what was happening in other years.

Parents were still an important part of the School 'family'. The PTA was

'Raising the roof' –
between two floors in 1984

thriving and showed its power and co-operation particularly during the Christmas Bazaar. This had been started chiefly through the enthusiasm of an Old Dolphin, Mary Price, in the first year of independence. It aimed, originally, to raise money for the Bursary Fund and became increasingly successful as one of the Godolphin and Latymer 'miracles'.

Starting a few weeks before the end of every November, it gathered strength slowly until, during the last week before the event when everyone was agreeing that it couldn't possibly be as good as the last one, it began to roll. As the bell rang for the end of school on the Friday afternoon before the day of the Bazaar, the action began. Drugget was laid in the gym to protect the floor, and then staff, Dolphins and their families set to work. Tables were carried from all over the School to be decorated for stalls. For many years, Christmas trees were bought (at reduced rates from a friendly wholesaler in Surrey who had grown up in Hammersmith) and stacked at the back of the

Girls produced Christmas cards to raise money for bursaries

114

hall so that the smell of pine joined with the sound of Christmas music as the Bazaar took shape.

There were inspired Christmas decorations, made by juniors, 'Portobello' bric-a-brac, 'This and That', home-made cakes, sweets, mountains of toys, the bottle stall, the Old Dolphins', the Bursary Fund and many others all coming to life. For 24 hours the cloisters housed one of the finest second-hand bookshops in West London. Staff and parents stood shoulder to shoulder in the dining-room, preparing and serving morning coffee and lunches. All the language departments had their own traditional attractions – a Parisian café, German Christmas spice cakes, Italian sweetmeats, Spanish sangria and Russian souvenirs. There were Christmas cards and calendars designed by girls – and these were only some of the fund-raising features.

Long queues waited for the doors to open on the Saturday morning and within a few hours of frenetic selling it was all over and, miraculously, the School looked like a school again instead of some wild Santa's cave.

The first Bazaar raised a remarkable £4,000 for the Bursary Fund and by 1994, after a succession of organisers including Gill Capel, Jean Glover and Sue Adey, it was netting £12,000, with much of the money divided between the Fund and outside charities. (Proceeds from the ODA Stall always stayed with the Bursary Fund.)

Hockey champions – 1980s

The world within the walls of the School was now humming with new ideas and new opportunities. In 1927 Sir William Bull, MP, then Chairman of the Governors, humorously observed that such were the expanding opportunities for women, now that they were getting the vote, that they might well live to see the day when the country had a woman Prime Minister. In 1979 Margaret Thatcher took over the government as Prime Minister. There had already been a landing on the moon. World communication by space satellite was thriving. It seemed that for women, at last, the opportunities were boundless.

Many VIth formers were now taking a year off between A Levels and University to explore the world, sending back long fragile air letters from remote places, reporting on the almost unbelievable responsibilities which they had taken on cheerfully within weeks of leaving school. The earliest of these journeys had been organised by VSO – Voluntary Service Overseas – but later, many girls preferred the shorter commitment of six to nine months

Lunch-time speaker David Puttnam with (front left) Katie Beckinsale, who asked him to talk about the cinema in 1985 (Courtesy Shepherds Bush Gazette)

offered by Project Trust and Operation Raleigh.

Typical of many was Alice Bulman, who went to help in a school in Africa and was offered the post of Head Mistress of the girls' section within three weeks of arriving there. She played a major part in reorganising the school – made arrangements for inter-school sports in the region, travelling with her teams over miles of rough country in an open lorry to take part in matches and competitions and, before returning to London, had managed to persuade the authorities to provide a permanent water supply for her pupils. (There was, she assured G & L, no truth in the rumour that this was known as 'Alice Springs'.)

Clare Hammond was sent with another girl to a Polio Rehabilitation Centre in Kingston, Jamaica, to set up goat's cheese production on an experimental farm and train workers, some of them handicapped, to take over when they left.

She wrote:

On our arrival we found 120 goats, two of which were named but the others unidentified, uncounted and as the kids were with their mothers until six months old, unmilked. Three bare rooms with ceiling tiles missing and no equipment... this was to be the dairy. Basically the herd had only been fed, watered and occasionally medicated whilst proliferating for the past three to four years.'

With the cool confidence of a true Dolphin, she continued, 'Our first couple of weeks were spent naming the goats, getting their description on paper, attempting to trace their parentages. We had no means of tagging them so naming them was the only alternative – from Azzelle and Battenburg through to Stripey when inspiration grew thin. Accurate descriptions entailed catching a goat (days spent doing flying tackles in large, dusty muck-scattered outdoor enclosures under the heat of the tropical sun) then hanging on to it ("oops, hey, look out! Mind the horns!")' The dairy roof was fixed – 'we removed every tile, cleaned both sides and then glued it back in place' and they travelled on public transport – 'usually jammed full to bursting with reggae music blaring out' to bludgeon the authorities to help them.

Before leaving they had rebuilt and reorganised a respectable dairy unit, reduced the size of the herd to a manageable 80 goats, produced cheese and yoghurt ('which met with great approval from the expatriate community but took Jamaicans a little longer – "how come it's no yellah? Wah, it's soft man"') and trained a local polio-handicapped girl to take over, 'giving her chemical understanding of how milk becomes cheese, making sure she knew why such procedures as sterilising and pasteurisation were necessary....' Clare returned home at the end of her year to read French and Chinese at Edinburgh University.

Sarah-Jane Rees receiving a cheque from money collected by G & L to help buy text books for her school of English in Guanaja, off Honduras – 1985 (Courtesy Richmond & Twickenham Times)

Sarah-Jane Rees spent eight months with a fellow volunteer on the remote island of Guanaja off the coast of Honduras, where their home was built on stilts to keep out the land crabs and hogs wandered through the tiny streets of the village – Savannah Bight. Between them, the two girls set up a school of English in a former café on the waterfront, making up their own curriculum, textbooks and exercises by the light of a hurricane lamp and teaching pupils from five-year-olds to grannies. Money from Godolphin's weekly Social Service collections as well as several cake sales was spent on buying text books on English for foreigners, which were sent out to Sarah-Jane, who, like Clare, taught the local youngsters to take over when the volunteers returned to England and, in her case, Oxford University.

Bridget O'Conor found herself bussing over deserts, flying in a five-seater plane and canoeing along swift-flowing rivers with a party of Operation Raleigh volunteers to help build a remote school in Peru, and carry out research into wild medicinal plants.

Sarah Wilson, as a Cambridge undergraduate, travelled to Nepal to carry out research into the potential for hydroelectric power which might improve the standard of living for the local people. (Her family later founded the Wilson Lectures, which take place annually.)

From the world outside, the Lunch Time Lectures tradition was established at about this time. Experts ranging from the politician Ken Livingstone to the film-producer David Puttnam were welcomed, and the hall was packed for their talks.

Between all the work there was always time for celebrating, and after marking the 21st birthday by opening the Godolphin Library, the 50th Jubilee was commemorated with a service at St Martin-in-the-Fields followed by a luncheon at Hammersmith Town Hall. The 75th occurred during Barbara Dean's term of office and was marked not only with the now traditional luncheon but also an assortment of souvenirs, including aprons with a picture of the School on the front, pens, dolphin paper-clips, and a stoneware mug designed by fourteen-year-old Rosie Reeve and made by Dunoon Potteries.

To the end of her life's work at Godolphin, Barbara Dean concentrated all her attention on the School, explaining that while she respected those who worked for education in the wider field, she felt that this was not the way for her personally.

There is no doubt that her loyalty, her great flair for organisation, her prodigious memory for all that needed to be done and her overwhelmingly gentle kindness and efficiency were responsible for Godolphin and Latymer's smooth successful change from maintained to independent status.

Again, there was great sadness and many gifts, including a music centre, when she retired at Christmas 1985.

11

NINETY YEARS ON

Margaret Rudland was still only thirty-nine years old when the Governors appointed her to replace Barbara Dean. Her qualifications were all they could have wished for and, added to that, her first post as a qualified teacher had been in the Mathematics Department at G & L, so she understood the ethos and atmosphere of the School.

Her own early education had been in a coeducational maintained school in Rayleigh, Essex, before she went on to read Mathematics and Physics at London University and take a postgraduate teacher-training course.

Although she had not grown up intending particularly to become a teacher, her cousin was a head mistress and she herself had always appreciated the help and care she had received during her own school life. When a vacancy for a Mathematics teacher at Godolphin and Latymer was advertised in *The Times Educational Supplement*, she applied, was interviewed by Margaret Gray in what is now her own office and felt immediately that she would enjoy working here.

'I had a Head of Department who pushed me, which was good training, the girls were clever and the atmosphere wonderful', she recalled, but after three years, she decided to sample life abroad and spent 15 months in Nigeria with VSO as Head of the Mathematics Department as well as teaching Physics and English at the Government Secondary School in Ilorin, Kwara State, with 50 pupils and one textbook to a class. Later, she became a School Inspector for Kwara State and travelled to several other schools.

Back in Britain, she taught briefly at Clapham County School in 1970–71 before joining the staff of St Paul's Girls' School, where she was Second Mistress for four years (on a rotational basis) and then became Head of Mathematics. After 11 years, she left to become Deputy Head of Norwich High School (1983–85).

One of her nostalgic ambitions for many years had been to become Head of Godolphin and Latymer, and although the chance presented itself sooner than she had expected, she applied for the post and was delighted to be appointed.

It was no easy task. Unlike her predecessors, she had no time to settle in quietly. The new GCSE courses were due to be introduced in the following September in preparation for the first examinations in 1988. 'Heads have always been warned to make no changes during their first year', she said, 'but I had no option. They were thrust upon us from outside in the form of the new style of examination and a new style of teaching'.

For some time the National Curriculum had been debated throughout the country amid considerable controversy. As an independent school, Godolphin followed it to some extent but was glad to be free of the restrictions which applied in the maintained sector. These meant that in addition to French and German it was still able to teach Latin, Greek, Russian, Spanish and Italian, none of which was among the essential 'core' subjects in maintained schools.

By 1995 the scheme had reached the end of its consultation period and Godolphin had built up its own 'core' of English, English Literature, Mathematics, Dual Award Sciences (Physics, Chemistry and Biology) and a modern language. Most girls were taking nine subjects, which left them able to choose a further three from a long list, in addition to the 'core'.

Throughout the 90 years of its existence the School had always been seeking out more space. The roof extension of the 1980s was already filled to overflowing by the time of its official opening, and even before Margaret Rudland had taken over as Head Mistress, the architect, Hans Haenlein, had been asked to undertake a review of the loading on each classroom. The needs identified for the future building were more Science laboratories, Art studios and better facilities for the staff to work.

The biggest problem, yet again, was where to build. In the end, the Governors, led by their Chairman Lady Goodison, accepted Haenlein's £3,000,000 scheme, which involved gutting Dame Joyce's 'new' Science block, knocking down part of the end of the Godolphin Library (to the grief of the Old Dolphins, but the memorial plaque to Miss Zachary was repositioned), razing the comparatively new Art, Music and VIth form building and encroaching on part of the Games area.

Shrewd and expert handling of the School's limited funds by the Finance Committee, which had managed to pay for the roof extension in the old building, was not going to provide all the necessary cash for this. Accordingly, a Building Appeal was launched to raise the extra £500,000 needed.

The Bursary Fund Appeal, so brilliantly directed by Margaret Gray in the late 1970s, had been successful in attracting many contributions from major companies, but some 20 years on there were so many good causes seeking grants from any possible source that appeals mostly fell on hard ground. It was the dedication of the staff, parents, pupils and, above all, the Old Dolphins, which successfully provided the bulk of the half-million pounds.

The girls again organised a succession of invaluable and inspired fundraising events; parents, grandparents and friends covenanted cash or paid it by other tax-saving methods; the Home Economics Department held a special dinner and the PTA organised an auction of gifts and promises which raised a resounding £22,000. This event was divided into two sections – a traditional auction of items which had been donated and a silent auction in which details of a different collection of lots were entered on lists pinned to the walls. Bidders entered their increasing amounts until the end of the evening, when the highest bidder won.

The catalogue reflected the still varied background of many of the Dolphins, ranging from offers of two hours' ironing or three hours' gardening to jewellery, paintings, the use of a luxury flat in Switzerland or a week in a country cottage.

Some of the liveliest bidding of the evening burst out when the auctioneer reached the lot offering the services of the Head Mistress to clean one car. Such was the enthusiasm that, in the excitement, two bids were accidentally accepted. Margaret Rudland solved the dilemma by agreeing to clean both. Only later did she admit, 'I cleaned one car – not very well because I forgot the windscreen – but I was delighted when they produced the second one and it turned out to be a Dinky toy'.

Once more following the tradition of keeping in touch with families, she added, 'It is a delight to work with the PTA. They support all our events with enthusiasm, particularly the Christmas Bazaar, the Jumble Sale, the tennis evening in the summer, the second-hand uniform sale and many more. They all bring many benefits to us, not only financially but through our warm contacts with so many homes'.

Fund-raising for the new building continued for several years but, slowly, the target was reached. Meanwhile, the bulldozers and the giant cranes had moved in and once more the staff and girls gritted their teeth for the months of building work, noise and dust which lay ahead.

The result has given the School a strong contrast in architectural styles between the Victorian Gothic of the main building and the sharply modern lines of the 1980s. The bricks were chosen with extreme care. Lady Goodison was particularly concerned that the colour should blend with the main School and admitted that for months she had found herself constantly looking at bricks on buildings and realising for the first time how different they could be.

The new Science/Arts building was formally opened in 1990 by a Godolphin parent, The Rt Hon. Christopher Patten, MP, shortly before he left to become the last Governor of Hong Kong.

Science teaching had always been innovative at G & L. The Nuffield Sciences had offered a very practical and investigative approach and the old laboratories were well-equipped, but the School simply did not have enough space for all science lessons to be timetabled in a laboratory. The new GCSE courses could not have Science lessons divided into practical and theory; practical work was essential for every lesson. This was particularly true for Advanced Level Sciences too, and now it had been provided, with ten new and well-equipped laboratories.

In place of the 'botanical garden' where the earliest Dolphins pored over plant life and bees, which had long disappeared, there was a new ecology garden, complete with a pond, where the girls could study the variety and development of plants without having to travel to sites across London.

Art, always popular in the School, with many girls continuing the subject to Advanced Level and going on to Foundation Courses at art school, had managed for years in cramped quarters. Now there were two studios for work up to GCSE, a separate room where VIth form artists could leave their work between lessons, a History of Art lecture room and photography studio, which quickly proved popular. The existing pottery studio with its old lead benches and its kilns stayed in the last remnant of the earliest Science laboratories behind the VIth form garden and the kitchen, providing a mellow background for the ecology area.

The Home Economics Department, moved from its original site behind the gym, now had not only a brand new teaching area with up-to-the-minute equipment but a separate room for theoretical work. (This was also used by some older girls for informal lunch-time lessons in making their own, up-to-the-minute clothes.)

What had been the Home Economics room now became a new, flexible and intimate Drama Workshop – again, much used.

Dame Joyce Bishop's pride, her new Science block, was transformed into a Music Department. In place of the laboratories there were two large studios and several small rooms for instrumental lessons, all in constant use as more and more girls entering the School were either already learning or wanting to take up a first or second instrument. As a result, the School benefited from more chamber and ensemble groups and more informal concerts, as well as the regular major music events.

The top floor main laboratory became a staff study plus two extra class-rooms and several administrative offices.

In fact, the whole decade between 1985 and 1995 saw tremendous changes, not just in facilities but in the subjects themselves – some, though not all of them, welcomed by the teaching staff.

The introduction of GCSE has led to a shift in emphasis in many disciplines and a broadening of the range of skills required of students at sixteen.

Writing at the time of the 90th birthday, some Heads of Department explained about the fundamental changes which have affected them.

In English, for example, oral work is now recognised as being important and a greater variety of writing is being undertaken rather than the combination of essay, comprehension and summary or directed writing which was so characteristic of O Level. The concept of the set texts remains but there is considerable flexibility of teacher choice, provided that certain core requirements are met. Another big change is the concession allowing students to take annotated texts into the examination.

In Mathematics, O Level has been replaced by a constantly changing series of syllabuses for the teaching of GCSE and then the National Curriculum (considered a great improvement on GCSE). Many people mourned the loss of some of the more rigorous aspects of O Level work, and students, nationally, are no longer expected to have such a thorough preparation for A Level or, indeed, studies in higher education. However, Godolphin and Latymer still tries to give its pupils a thorough grounding in those topics, such as Algebra, which has suffered some decline, whilst, at the same time, embracing the newer aspects of courses such as statistics and coursework.

Science reported 'tremendous upheavals' in Physics, Chemistry and Biology, with coursework assessment and the three disciplines being taken by every girl to GCSE. The School follows a course in which girls no longer gain individual subject awards in the three subjects but a final double grade (the Dual Award) which encompasses their overall achievements. There have been changes too in A Level Chemistry and Biology, with coursework assessment replacing the traditional three-hour practical examinations.

In Modern Languages there has been a great move away from the written to the spoken language and more emphasis placed on contemporary society and current events than on literary tests.

Although Godolphin has a long tradition of encouraging as many school visits abroad as possible, the past ten years has seen an increase in the range of these and a greater concentration on achieving a working knowledge of the language and culture of countries. From the time they enter the School, all girls have a chance to travel, to France and later on the exchange visits to the Johanneum in Hamburg, to Paris and more recently to Moscow and New York, where there are established exchange schemes. Students of Spanish have stayed with families in Spain; the Art staff are still taking groups regularly to the museums and galleries of Italy, Holland and France and the Physical Education Department is travelling with teams to contests abroad. Added to these are ski trips for sheer pleasure during the spring term.

Small wonder that many Old Dolphins travel throughout the world from the moment they end their school life.

History no longer starts with the Stone Age, working its way through a list of dates to be learned by heart. Pupils are, instead, encouraged to adopt the kind of approach used by professional historians, examining evidence (sometimes conflicting) and drawing conclusions from it.

The inclusion of coursework as a significant part of many GCSE and A Level courses has led to greater flexibility and, perhaps, fairer, more continuous assessment of achievement.

It is possible in some subjects such as Home Economics or Geography for girls to pursue topics of their own choice, and these can be stimulating and exciting. In Home Economics, for instance, which deals now with nutrition, investigation, recipe development and the use of time- and labour-saving equipment, highlight of recent years for the new UIII has been a 'Godolphin and Latymer Masterchef' competition. For the UIV it came with the 'mini-enterprise' in which groups planned their own restaurant, complete with name, logo, uniforms and a menu of mouth-watering dishes, while VIth formers could opt to take a short course on planning a sensible grant-conscious diet for when they left home to study in higher education.

Interpreting satellite maps, computing and word processing are all fundamental topics in modern Geography, with fieldwork and residential courses still a vital part of the syllabus after a dramatic transition in 1988 from GCE to GCSE. The new course is designed to encourage the development of a wide range of skills and to encompass key ideas, including population and settlement resources and economic activities, physical environment and human activities and development.

In practice, this includes researching such topics as whether Heathrow needs a fifth terminal and where, in a small garden or the School grounds, is the best place for a seat. Both of these are equally acceptable to examiners as long as they have a spatial element and are related to the GCSE course. To help with studies, a weather station has been installed on the School roof to record all aspects of the weather every hour of every day and relay it to a terminal in the computer room. Within months of this equipment being established, the School was selected to take part in a survey on air quality in London, carried out by London University.

Dolphins are still able to study a wide range of subjects, including such 'non-core' languages as Latin and Ancient Greek, plus Classical Civilisation to GCSE and A Level and Ancient History to A Level. Economics is a VIth form option, with more emphasis on markets and less on government intervention than previously. It was brought up to date in 1995 by the introduction into the National Syllabus of an option paper on economic development which focuses on the less developed countries and the emerging markets of Eastern Europe. More attention is paid to such topical and controversial issues as health economics and transport to help students understand the issues involved in the current economic debates and view them objectively.

Following a trend which started in the 1960s, the GCSE and the new A Level courses in Music have gone through a minor revolution with the emphasis changed to make it much more a practical and creative subject. Students are expected to try their hand at composing right from the start instead of attempting it after a thorough grounding in musical theory, harmony and counterpoint. Performing is now recognised as an essential element of Music in the classroom and a compulsory part of GCSE and A Level – a change from the days when a student could pass an O Level without playing or singing a note. Classes study a wider variety of music, not only classical but jazz and pop. The Head of Music predicts that the use of information technology in the composition and notating of music is likely to open a whole new world of possibilities for musical education in the future.

Religious Studies would hardly be recognisable to the original Dolphin boys, struggling to learn their Catechism and chunks of the Bible by heart. One can imagine their reaction to the news that in 1993 and 1995, the Head of Religious Studies took a party of his pupils to the Sinai desert, where, travelling on camels, they explored biblical history at first hand.

The subject now emphasises an approach which examines the roots of religious beliefs and institutions and the political, cultural and economic causes behind their development. A tradition of the study of Philosophy has taken root in the School. For non-examination students, modern issues in religion, ethics and social change can be studied, along with the emergence of cults and new religious movements – about which they need to be well-informed.

Even Physical Education has changed beyond anything the enthusiastic young women who 'bowled underarm' and 'played the game' could have believed possible in the School's early days.

The past problems of the playing-field, with its couch grass and potato planting, through its aircraft factory and tomato-growing to the more recent mud in wet winters, have been forgotten. In 1993 the whole field was dug to a depth of a metre as the contractors moved in to instal Astroturf, an artificial grass surface. Despite the girls' fears that this would mean the end of traditional sunbathing on the grass, the pitch was transformed into a hockey pitch for the winter and nine extra tennis courts for summer.

The PE Department now teaches table-tennis, rounders, health-related fitness and aerobics as well as hockey, tennis and gymnastics in its programme for the nineties and on into the 21st century. Girls are introduced to the fitness room with all its equipment and the Astroturf was reported to be 'having a quite stunning effect on hockey and tennis standards, especially at the lower end of the School'.

These are all part of the curriculum but in addition, there is an assortment of extra-curricular activities. Fencing takes place in School and squash is offered at the Broadway Squash Club. Other activities, added in the early 90s, are yoga, jazz dance, rowing, scuba diving and snorkelling, tennis coaching from outside professionals, plus gym, dance, badminton, rounders and table-tennis clubs and an aerobics class where the teaching staff can join in with the VIth formers.

The real value of all this is in the obvious enthusiasm and enjoyment throughout the School – for both girls and staff.

Many girls take part in the Duke of Edinburgh's Award Scheme, which was started in the School in 1989. In June 1993, five girls, Rosalind Chin, Chloe Garrow, Rebecca Groocock, Rosie Millar and Katie Streatfeild, received Gold Awards from the Duke of Edinburgh in a ceremony at St James's Palace. It was a 'first' for the School and rare for as many as five 'Golds' to be awarded simultaneously to candidates from the same school.

Drama has developed rapidly since the appointment of Mick Fitzmaurice as a specialist teacher and the School plays have progressed from the Cockpit productions with smaller casts, to bigger events. *Percy Mercer's Circus* was performed at the Cochrane Theatre in 1987, in co-operation with the Music Department, and in 1990, *Vackees*, a musical based on the wartime evacuation of children from London, was staged at the Westminster Theatre and later, at the Lyric, Hammersmith. Another musical – *Roll Up! Roll Up!*, the story of animals who wanted to run away from a circus – was produced with great success and professional enthusiasm at the Lyric in 1995. For several years, Dolphins have taken their own productions to the 'fringe' at the Edinburgh Festival and revelled in good reviews.

Following tradition, the Lower Vth and VIth forms still have their own plays, produced with the help of Mick Fitzmaurice; and the LIV–UIV Form Play Competition still goes ahead, with the plays written and produced by VIth formers.

Christmas brings the traditional UIII pantomime for local elderly people as part of their annual party – from which they stagger home laden with parcels of festive food.

Early in the ninth decade, the Carol Service, with choir, orchestra and organ, finally outgrew the School hall and was moved to St Paul's Church on Hammersmith Broadway. The singers still arrive and leave in procession, holding candles which flicker down the darkened aisles. Traditionalists miss the waning sound of voices echoing through empty classrooms as the singers slowly move away into the distance down the lower corridor, but admit that the new service is a moving and heart-warming symbol that Christmas has, indeed, arrived.

No London school (and few in the country) can escape from the pressures being aimed at teenagers these days, and in 1995 the School Forum was dissolved. In its place, a School Council was established to give all the pupils a democratic voice in the School. Guidelines and membership were carefully thought out by Sophie Clarke, the Head Girl in 1994–5, and her team, so that each year has a representative and the whole School and staff are welcomed at its meetings.

In early 1995 the Council considered the question of school uniform. They also discussed theft and bullying and were drafting documents setting out their views, to be given to all new girls entering the School so that they would understand its ethos.

Uniform has been a problem for many years. Gone are the days when the hatband was a subject of awe and respect. Gone, indeed, are the hats. The grey uniform topcoats were expensive and anything which might single girls out in a crowd during their journeys to and from School was considered inadvisable. Topcoats are now optional black or grey, or a red cagoule.

(Out of concern for the girls' safety, the School has developed a Common Sense Defence course for the youngest pupils when they first enter the School.)

Clothes to wear to school are turning full circle, with pressure growing for a return to the original system in 1905 of no uniform at all, other than for games.

Many of the earliest pupils had liked the idea of a uniform so much that they wore their navy blue pleated tunics in School as well as on the field, and until the 1930s the prospectus advised that the only essential uniform was a hat (straw boaters at first, with elastic under the chin, followed by panama in summer and felt in winter) all encircled by the essential blue and white hatband. In Miss Zachary's time, most of the girls wore the navy, box-pleated tunic with a white blouse, some with a 'Peter Pan' collar, others with a collar and tie. Miss Bishop (inevitably!) modernised it all, bringing in the then fashionable 'princess line' navy tunic with a white square-neck blouse.

It was only after the war, towards the end of Dame Joyce's period as Head Mistress, that the navy tunic gave way to a grey skirt and the square-neck blouse was replaced by a turquoise blouse. This, too, was abandoned when problems arose with the dye, and the uniform shirt is now a fine stripe in the School colours of red and white. Summer dresses in crisp pink, grey or turquoise gingham were dismissed as 'looking like tablecloths' in the 1990s, when the girls voted to change them for a 'Gothic-Look' black and white, in keeping with the general student fashion for sombre black at all times. The short-lived grey beret of the 1950s and 60s has long since vanished.

Scarlet for games goes back to the 1930s, when the School teams wore red tunics, which later changed to divided skirts.

By the 1990s, an added pressure for schools appeared on the scene with the arrival of a new phenomenon, fostered by the media – The Schools League Tables. Each year, statistics are produced ranking schools nationally, according to their successes at GCSE and Advanced Level.

With its customary excellent level of marks, Godolphin and Latymer comes high on these national lists, but Margaret Rudland makes her feelings clear: 'I hope that I am successful in convincing prospective parents that such tables only reflect a slice of life in the School. They must visit us with their daughters to sense the atmosphere, the vitality and the friendliness. I hope that all girls who come here will feel part of a lively community and take their academic work comfortably while still having time and spare capacity and interest for clubs and societies, sports, drama and music'.

There is still great competition for entry, with five eager applicants for every place available in the annual intake of just over 100.

The spiritual side of the School remains important, but every Assembly no longer involves squashing the entire School of 700 bodies into the hall. Instead, there are now junior and senior assemblies on different days, but the whole School continues to come together – still hopelessly squashed – on Monday mornings to pause, however briefly, for spiritual refreshment and a chance to think quietly.

With the many problems facing families and the enormous outside pressures on young people, the School decided, in the early 1990s, to employ a counsellor to help any girl who might feel the need to seek advice or talk through her problems with an expert on an entirely confidential basis. Several years previously, a full-time nurse had been provided to deal immediately with accidents or any ailment or illness.

The 1990s have been a period of increasing unemployment and uncertainty so that first-class careers advice has been essential. Over the past 30 years this has been part of G & L life, with staff helping out and a close affinity, thanks to Margaret Gray's connection, with the National Advisory Centre on Careers for Women. Parents and Old Dolphins visit the School to help with Careers Weeks and, under the guidance of Julie Kaiser, a careers room and a full and expert careers advice network have been established. This has been expanded with weekly talks about their own work by an assortment of speakers and these are open to the whole School. Particular guidance is given to girls when they are choosing GCSE, Advanced Level or Higher Education courses. By the beginning of the 1990s the work experience scheme for UV, which for some years was London-orientated had been expanded, in co-operation with Latymer Upper School, to include experience for VIth formers in Paris and Berlin, with the work ranging from law, medicine and business to TV camera crewing and hotel management.

Two sad events and one joyful one marked the decade after Margaret Rudland took office. For nearly five years, the School had enjoyed the company of four out of its six Head Mistresses, but in the autumn of 1989, only four years after her retirement, Barbara Dean died. On 21 November a Thanksgiving Service for the life and work which she had dedicated to Godolphin and Latymer for so many years was held in a crowded St Peter's Church, Hammersmith, the scene of so many School Birthdays in happier times. The senior choir sang 'Laudamus Te' from Vivaldi's *Gloria* and 'How Lovely Are Thy Dwellings Fair' from the Brahms Requiem, and the junior choir sang 'O Lovely Peace' from Handel's *Judas Maccabeus*. At her request, John Bunyan's words 'Who would true valour see' were sung by the congregation before a reading from *Pilgrim's Progress* and later, an extract from *Little Gidding* by T S Eliot on the importance of prayer. Margaret Gray praised all that Barbara had done for the school and her quiet, lifelong dedication. The service ended with Sir Francis Drake's prayer, which Miss Dean had repeated so often in Assembly and which was always associated with her:

O Lord God, when Thou givest to Thy servants to endeavour any great matter, grant us to know that it is not the beginning but the continuing of the same until it be thoroughly finished, which yieldeth the true glory: through Him that for the finishing of Thy work laid down His life, Thy Son, Jesus Christ. Amen.

Dame Joyce seemed destined to live for ever. Even in her nineties with increasing deafness and failing sight, she would sit each morning while Elizabeth Ellett read *The Times* to her, and then launch herself into the outside world again for anything from walking the latest in a long succession of small dogs round the block near her home to attending meetings or reunions from some of the many organisations or Old Dolphins with whom she kept in constant and enthusiastic contact. 'Night time is the worst', she would explain. 'Now that I can no longer see to read in bed the time passes very slowly, but I am thankful that I was encouraged to learn so many poems when I was at school and now I can, at least, recite them to while away the time until morning'.

Death came swiftly after she developed pneumonia in hospital following a fall at her home a few days before her 97th birthday in July, 1993. Her many friends were deeply shocked and plans were laid to honour her remarkable life with a Memorial Service.

St Margaret's Church, Westminster, was packed to the doors, with the congregation including not only many old friends and former pupils but the entire first year of Godolphin and Latymer, the School choirs and several of its leading music students.

The choir sang the Introit 'Drop down, ye heavens' from Isaiah 45:8, and Psalm 85:10–11, and among those who took part in the service were Lady Goodison, who read from the Wordsworth sonnets 'Still glides the Stream'; Margaret Rudland, who read the verses from Ecclesiasticus 44 'Let us now praise famous men...'; and Sir Henry Brooke (son of Lady Brooke), who read from Romans 12:1–9. Margaret Gray, gave an Address, praising Dame Joyce for the many great achievements of her life and concluding: 'Joyce was a true enhancer of life, bringing the best out of thousands of people, loving and loved by her ex-pupils and the many, many friends with whom she kept in touch through a huge correspondence.

'We who knew her in later years think of her most in her own home in Putney. We see her, beautifully dressed, with immaculate hair, a broad smile on her face and a friendly dog at her feet – welcoming us in. Looking 20 years younger than her age, disregarding her increasing blindness, treating us to racy talk, salty anecdotes, amiable gossip, occasional exasperated ragings at the follies of planners and theorists, she remained to the end a splendid hostess and a dear companion'.

The service, which had included a thunderous rendering of the hymn *All my hope on God is founded*, ended with the traditional *God be in my head and in my understanding* before the hundreds of her friends filed through to the nearby Westminster School for a reception in her memory.

On a lighter note, the School celebrated Margaret Gray's eightieth birthday with a special lunch in the School hall for many of her friends and relations. Lady Goodison welcomed the guests and, after the meal, there was a concert of music, Shakespearian speeches and a modern monologue from Stephen Jeffrey's *Absent Friends*. Then the girls presented her with a birthday cake, gifts and flowers.

In her personal tribute, Margaret Rudland pointed out that Margaret Gray seemed to have embarked on a series of new careers since her retirement in 1973. She was now a Governor of Hampton School, both Francis Holland

130

Schools, West Heath School in Sevenoaks and the Unicorn School in Kew. She had continued as Chairman of NACCW and, every Monday, was to be found helping in her local Oxfam shop. 'Retirement', she vowed, 'is not for cissies'.

12

OLD DOLPHINS

Almost as soon as the first pupils reached the end of their School life, the Old Dolphins Association was founded in 1910; 'not at my instigation', as Miss Clement made clear, 'but at the demand of some Old Dolphins who claimed the right to connect themselves in some definite way with their old School. I meekly (and gladly) admitted their right; the Association came "into being" and although still young [she was writing in 1916] is strong and lusty. I have no doubt that if I had been importunate in urging and pressing girls to become members of our Association the membership (which stands now at the satisfactory figure of 206) might have been still higher, but then the voluntary spirit (so dear to the heart of Britishers) would have been missing and I have always held that if girls wish to belong to an Association of this kind, they should do so on their own initiative.... If the opportunity of keeping in touch with the School by returning to the old haunts and meeting old companions and mistresses is not in itself a sufficient inducement, girls are not likely to gain much from belonging to our Association'.

Little is known about the first few years, other than the fact that former pupils who lived near enough to the School came together for meetings from time to time, but in 1916 there were enough members to fund a leaflet. This was issued as often as possible and gives an insight into what happened to Dolphins when they left in those days. It also made it clear that these were not simply meetings to chat and discuss business but there was a thriving weekly Old Dolphin gym class as well as OD hockey and netball teams which played other schools' former pupils and, at times, the School teams. There were also well-attended lectures, with such tantalising titles as 'The Duties, Hopes and Fears of Women Clerks'.

By 1917 the leaflet was including lists of University entrances and successes and there was a call for an Honours Board to be placed in the School hall, with the hope that this would be made possible 'after the war'. There was also a list of the present names and addresses of paid-up ODs.

The war – the 'Great War' – of 1914–18 affected many members of the Association who were either working in government departments or serving as nurses or in WAACS – the Women's Auxiliary Army Corps. Those who stayed at home and could still attend ODA meetings not only raised the money to support the School's room at the Star and Garter Home but gave dances and concerts, organised a War Trophies Exhibition and held Dolphin flag days to buy wool, which, reported the 1917 leaflet, 'was quickly knitted into socks, mufflers, caps and mittens. The total number of articles sent to the Comforts Depot, to the Red Cross Society and for minesweepers on the Suffolk coast is 559'. Dolphin flag days seem to have been a regular means of fund-raising, but no trace of the flags has survived.

Later, the Old Dolphins decided that some sort of fund should be started to help those who had fallen on hard times after leaving School, however long ago they had left, or even for pupils in the School who needed help urgently.

From this, in 1931, grew the Franc Ha Leal Fund, which, for many years, was boosted by an annual summer fête and by small envelopes tucked in with School reports, soliciting a contribution.

Until 1987, it was up to every girl who left School to decide whether or not she wanted to join the Association, but from that time, a life membership was included in the School fees for all but a few who preferred to opt out. A database was established in a special ODA office, organised by Caroline Shattock, an Old Dolphin with a daughter in the School, and by 1995 there were 1,600 members and a growing interest in returning to meet old friends.

All receive two 'mailings' of news a year, one of which includes the School Magazine, with an Old Dolphin section. Often in the past there were complaints that it was not worth attending meetings because there was no guarantee that there would be anyone else around from the same year. This has been put right by the organising of special 'year' reunions.

But after such a full school life, what happens to ODs? How many, as some visitors to the School enquire, are famous?

The answer must be 'not a lot', but followed by the argument 'what is fame and how much does it matter?' One can't help feeling that it is ironic and somehow true to the Godolphin spirit that the name which brings the most immediate recognition is Hattie Jacques, comedienne and star of films and TV, the girl who spent much of her school life struggling with her fat problem and wanting desperately to go on the stage.

On the 'fame' side currently, there is Dr Susan Greenfield, the brilliant scientist who fascinated the nation with her Christmas Lectures from the Royal Institution in 1994–5; actresses Samantha Bond and Kate Beckinsale; Sarah ('Linda' at school) Dunant, TV presenter, novelist and scriptwriter; journalist Nigella Lawson; distinguished professional pianist Kathron Sturrock; Vastiana Belfon, who went to Oxford and later became presenter of the TV programme *Ebony*; Lindsey Beaven, whose tennis skills took her as far as the Wimbledon tournaments; Rachel Squire – Labour MP for Dunfermline; Tau Tau Liu, who made a memorable impact on School drama and became the first woman Dean of Wadham College, Oxford; Daphne Clark, M.B.E., founding spirit and for many years Director of the Richmond-Upon-Thames Churches Housing Trust, which provides homes for so many homeless people. She is also one of the leading experts on housing trusts in Britain.

Dolphins remember sadly, too, Julie Tullis (née Palau), climber, professional photographer and the first Briton to conquer K2, who died of frostbite and exhaustion when the expedition was overtaken by a long, severe storm during the descent in August 1986. (Her book *Clouds from Both Sides* was published in 1988.) Also Cassandra ('Casso') Clunies-Ross, always deeply concerned with conservation, who died when the light aircraft carrying her to inspect a forest crashed in the jungle on a remote Pacific Island.

But there are, by now, thousands more, all over the world, whose less dramatic lives have been influenced not only by the lessons but by the whole background and atmosphere of G & L and who look back on it with nostalgia and, from time to time, return after anything up to 75 years.

On the School's 50th Birthday many ODs sent in their memories to be included in the Jubilee history of the School. These were so interesting and gave such a flavour of School life over the years from the other side of the blackboard that it seemed worth including a brief selection from them, along with others collected more recently.

1905–6. 'The new building, so very clean and new and handsome. Wonderful furniture. Desks carefully adjusted to our persons at the beginning of each term.... It was said to be the best equipped girls' school in London. The labs – quite wonderful for a girls' school. The unusual Art room planned by Miss Edith Clement (sister of the Head Mistress). The botanical gardens where we tended specimens for Miss Jackson. The initials cut in the brick walls of the field – presumably those of boys in the preceding school...'

1906 – the first School Birthday. 'The march of the aborigines was particularly popular...'

'The additions to the School in 1909 which account for the apparently capricious system of numbering the rooms.'

'The setting out of a sort of tuck-shop on trestle tables, stocked by Erbach's of King Street – most delicious cakes and buns and doughnuts with glasses of hot milk if liked...'

'The diabolo contest on the asphalt playground in 1908.'

'The snowball fight on the mistresses' tennis court in 1909.'

'The respect paid to the School hatband...'

'Gloves were not optional...'

'The moth-bally smell in the red tunics worn by members of the School hockey and netball teams. They had double rows of buttons to let down for the taller ones.'

'Sports Days including mass drill by girls in white hats and white shoes, figure marching accompanied by the Grand March from *Tannhäuser* and the terrible anxiety borne by those who formed the human revolving wheel.'

'The first skipping competition – the crisp thwack of skipping ropes in a hall tense with excitement on skipping competition days.' (For many years, skipping was a compulsive pastime – many ODs ask if it still takes place and are disappointed to hear that it is virtually unheard of in the modern G & L.)

'Growing plants for the bulb and flower shows.'

'The pleasures of learning about the mysteries of bee-keeping on a sunny summer afternoon, or of hearing the hum of bees among the flowers.'

1914–18. 'Parties for Belgian refugees; demonstrations of vaulting on the field for wounded soldiers; air raids in 1917 – the air raid maroons sounded during the dinner hour and the whole dining population took cover in the lower corridor.... Miss Mayor taking groups of girls across to Paris in the early 1920s and bringing back orange braid for our games "bands".'

'The first London Schools' Music Festival in 1927 when the Upper School choir gained first place in the first class, singing Pergolesi's *Stabat Mater* choruses.'

'The facilities for Science which were uncommon in girls' schools in 1930 – Zoology was very unusual then and there were still many schools where Botany was the only Science...'

'Watching proudly when Miss Bryan captained the All-England Hockey team.'

'The terrible feeling of aloneness as I left School to be evacuated.'

'Knowing we were secure in the charge of Miss Bishop and the staff and therefore accepting the probability of war and all it entailed quite philosophically.'

'The unique experience of continuing lessons as though everything were normal when the School building had been shattered by bomb blast.'

'The 50th Birthday Service at St Martin in the Fields and the luncheon afterwards.'

'Wonderful School plays, Christmas carols and tableaux.'

'Singing and form play competitions.'

'School Birthday Services – at St John's Church beside the School, at St Peter's and at St Paul's, Hammersmith Broadway.'

'The farewell parties for Dame Joyce, for Miss Gray and Miss Dean.'

135

'Marching on Parliament with our dolphin banners to save Godolphin and being mistaken for "Save the Whales".'

'A Level examinations in the gym in 1976 when the temperature was 32 degrees centigrade.'

'The all-time record screams which greeted Mr Escott when he appeared in the staff play on the School Birthday, dressed in silver as David Bowie and singing "Ground Control to Major Tom".'

And memories in 1995 still of: 'being terrified of Miss Zachary'. Or, alternatively:

'Miss Zachary's graciousness, her calm way of dealing with us, her elegance, droll sense of humour and her kindness, but the occasional surprise. When my mother said I wanted to be a poultry farmer she exclaimed, 'Oh Mrs Hows, not those lousy chickens".'

'At the "Little School" in the bombing when Miss Pocock would insist on taking us all home – however far that was – to make sure that we got back safely when bombs were disrupting the railways and buses.'

'Drinking from our third-of-a-pint milk bottles at break in the freezing cloisters before they were glassed in – and using the cold and draughty toilets there.'

'Misbehaving and always being caught because I was the one with red hair.'

'Losing my prefect's badge for talking in the library. Getting my prefect's badge back because I was then the only girl in the VIth without some sort of badge.'

'Enjoying being slightly shocked to see Miss Dean (then Head of History) playing Bottom in the staff play on the Birthday and Miss Gray – the Head Mistress – wearing trousers as she rode round the drive in circles on the bicycle we have given her for her retirement – and what a wonderful send-off we gave her!'

'Going to our first Latin lesson when the mistress told us that *Defende nobis juvenes Malos, Deus benigne* in the School Hymn meant "Lord, defend us from bad young men".'

'The mischievous American girl ("Jest call me Tammy!") who locked a teacher in a cupboard and although we could hear the calls for help we were so horrified we just froze!'

'Being terribly sad at leaving. If I ever drive through Hammersmith I always go up Iffley Road to look at the School and think "I'm so glad that I went there".'

EPILOGUE

For Margaret Rudland, the past ten years have been the busiest of her life. Her love of travelling has blossomed with visits abroad, to Russia, where she has established a firm friendship with the Head of the Moscow exchange school and her family; to Hamburg and our Johanneum friends; to China and India to examine their education systems at first hand and, on the rare occasion, to France for a rest or to enjoy her hobby of opera.

Her particular interest in education has been encouraged by the Governors and supported by the teaching staff. From 1989 to 92 she was Chairman of the Joint Standing Committee of the Girls' School Association and the Independent Association of Preparatory Schools. From 1989 she was a member of the Council of the Girls' School Association (London Region) and from 1993 to 94 she Chaired the GSA Education Committee. In 1996 she is due to become President of the Girls' School Association.

Since 1990, too, she has enjoyed being a member of the Nightingale Fund Council, which meets three times a year to award money to nurses from Florence Nightingale's gifts from the nation.

Her comment on the state of Godolphin and Latymer in its 90th year? 'I hope it is well respected – I certainly hear many warm comments about it. There is no doubt that, like most other schools today, whether maintained or independent, there are worries, but I find many joys in the School which outnumber the problems. There's the liveliness, vigour and talent of the young, their ability to make you laugh (and occasionally, cry!) and their resilience.

'As to the future, there will need to be more building, not to increase the numbers but further to improve our facilities.

'Whatever other changes there are to come I hope that the essence of the School remains the same: friendly and welcoming yet purposeful and busy. I hope too that the School will continue to place value on the individual and the community, emphasising independence and service. Miss Zachary's aims for the School are mine too:

> – in essentials, unity
> in non-essentials, liberty
> in all things, charity'.

The Song of the Old Dolphins, lost now in the mists of time!

THE SCHOOL SONG (original version, 1912)

(This was revised later by Vera Titmuss, and was based, loosely, on the song outlining the daily duties of the monarch of Barataria in Gilbert & Sullivan's *The Gondoliers*. According to a magazine of 1891, Queen Victoria watched a performance of this in the Waterloo Gallery at Windsor Castle and enquired of Mr D'Oyly Carte the meaning of the interpolations.

'These, Your Majesty, are what we call "gags",' he replied.

'Gags!' replied the Queen. 'I thought gags were things that were put by authority into people's mouths.'

'These gags, Your Majesty,' answered the manager, bowing profoundly, 'are things that people put into their own mouths without authority.'

The Queen smiled benignly and seemed perfectly satisfied with the reply.

The Godolphin and Latymer version demands a degree of dash bordering on controlled rowdiness on occasions deemed to be unsuitable for the School Hymn and always during the afternoon entertainment on the School Birthday. By a tradition, built up over the years, the chorus is sung to the accompaniment of stamping feet and at increasing speed in the hope of beating the pianist to the final notes.

138

Rising early in the morning we proceed to Iffley Road
Every girl her head adorning with a school hat, new or old.
Each is fearful lest too late
She should come inside the gate.

On our pegs our hats and jackets
We suspend and then the packets
With our dinners we deposit on the shelves.
Then our bags we haste to carry
To our form rooms, if we tarry
Red marks we'll reap in plenty for ourselves.
So very soon our lessons have begun
And we hope we shan't forget them every one.
First of all we try to wrestle with some French
And then we have to give our minds a wrench
To penetrate the mystery of Elizabethan history
(It's a rather tiresome business we forget the names and dates).
Then the break bell makes us hurry
All is bustle, haste and scurry
To the table where we buy our buns and eat them without plates.
Thus refreshed, we go to battle
With hard problems about cattle –
If six cows could eat a bale of hay how much would sixty eat?
Spend a little time in singing
Or perhaps some moments clinging
To the ropes in the gymnasium
With the aid of hands and feet.
After dinner we may wander
Round the gardens and may ponder
On the orders and the habitats of plants.
If by chance the day be sunny
We can watch the bees make honey
And if the day be wet we love to dance.
But the bell rings loud and long at 2.15
And hard at work each girl may soon be seen
Some may learn how they should choose a piece of meat
And how to cook and make it fit to eat.
Others brush and pencil bearing
To the art room swift repairing
Draw and paint familiar objects (they can do it rather well).
Some spend afternoons at science
Learn to use each weird appliance
And on the air comes floating many a strange and wondrous smell.
After school it is a pleasure

To play hockey in full measure
Then we hurry to the cloisters, seize our bags, leave none behind.
If we do, we'll be suspended
And our pleasure will be ended
For a whole week – and it's better to be careful, so we find.

CHORUS:

So we hail the fourth of May
When we keep the School's birthday
With dance and song and music
And with celebrations meet.
'Tis a privilege and pleasure
That we treasure beyond measure
For the Dolphin School's delightful
And is very hard to beat.

THE SCHOOL SONG (1960s version)

Rising early in the morning we proceed to Iffley Road
Every girl herself adorning with a scarlet duffel hood.
      Each is fearful lest too late
      She should come inside the gate.
      By the Staff-room we foregather
      Or perchance to read the weather
(Take a friend along for luck in either case).
      When the dinner money's checked
      All the homework we collect
Alphabetically, every book in place.
So very soon our lessons have begun
We hope we shan't forget them every one.
First of all we try to wrestle with some French,
And then we have to give our minds a wrench
To penetrate the mystery of Elizabethan history;
It's a rather tiresome business, we forget the names and dates.
      Then the break bell makes us hurry
      All is bustle, haste and scurry
To the table where we drink our milk and eat our chocolate.
      Thus refreshed we go to battle
      With hard problems about cattle.
'If six cows could eat a bale of hay, how much could sixty eat?'
      Spend a little time in singing
      Or perhaps some minutes clinging
To the ropes in the gymnasium with the aid of hands and feet.

      There's a long, long queue for dinner
      (Every moment we feel thinner)
But we have a little gossip on the way.
      Then we eat our lunch and chatter
      (Every moment getting fatter)
Though there's never time for all we have to say.
But the bell rings loud and long at just 2.10
And hard at work each girl may soon be then.
Some learn how they should choose a piece of meat
And how to cook and make it fit to eat.
      Others, brush and pencil bearing
      To the Art Room swift repairing
Draw and paint familiar figures (they can do it rather well).
      Some spend afternoons at Science
      Learn to use each weird appliance
And on the air comes floating many a strange and wondrous smell.

After school it is a pleasure
To play hockey in full measure
Watch a match or practise singing, tune our fiddles, join debate.
Then in shower or rain or shine
For the bus or District Line
With our harrowing thoughts of homework we go hurrying through the gate.

CHORUS: So we hail the 4th of May
When we keep the School's birthday
With dance and song and music and with celebrations meet.
It's a privilege and pleasure
Which we treasure beyond measure
For the Dolphin School's delightful and it's very hard to beat.

INDEX